The Knowledge-Enabled Organization

The Knowledge-Enabled Organization

Moving From "Training" to "Learning" to Meet Business Goals

Daniel R. Tobin, Ph.D.

AMACOM
American Management Association

New York • Atlanta • Boston • Chicago • Kansas City • San Francisco • Washington, D.C.
Brussels • Mexico City • Tokyo • Toronto

This book is available at a special
discount when ordered in bulk quantities.
For information, contact Special Sales Department,
AMACOM, a division of American Management Association,
1601 Broadway, New York, NY 10019.

This publication is designed to provide accurate and authoritative
information in regard to the subject matter covered. It is sold with the
understanding that the publisher is not engaged in rendering legal,
accounting, or other professional service. If legal advice or other expert
assistance is required, the services of a competent professional person
should be sought.

Library of Congress Cataloging-in-Publication Data

Tobin, Daniel R., 1946–
    The knowledge-enabled organization : moving from "training" to
"learning" to meet business goals / Daniel R. Tobin.
        p.   cm.
    Includes bibliographical references and index.
    ISBN 0-8144-0366-2 (hardcover)
    1. Employees—Training of.   2. Employer-supported education.
I. Title.
HF5549.5.T7T596   1997
658.3'124—DC21   97-24846
                                                                CIP

Printing number

10   9   8   7   6   5   4   3   2   1

For
Susan
and
Molly

Contents

Acknowledgments

Throughout this book, I use many examples of excellent programs from a wide variety of companies. Many of these examples come from business literature, often enhanced by discussions or correspondence with managers of those exemplary programs. In several cases, I have been able to visit companies that are well on their way to becoming knowledge-enabled organizations. My thanks go out to Bob Buckman, chairman, Mark Koskiniemi, vice-president of human resources, and dozens of other people I interviewed at Buckman Laboratories, a specialty chemical company headquartered in Memphis, Tennessee. Our contact started with electronic mail messages and was followed by my three-day visit to their facilities. I also thank them for providing access to the company's knowledge network to see how it is really used. Mark Koskiniemi also provided invaluable assistance in reviewing the entire manuscript and offering insightful and valuable suggestions.

Hubert Saint-Onge hosted my visit to the leadership center for the Canadian Imperial Bank of Commerce (CIBC). Mr. Saint-Onge is a pioneer in many respects, especially in developing the concept of the "learning contract" and in setting one of the earliest examples I have found for destroying a company's training catalog. I thank him for allowing me to share some of CIBC's materials with the readers of this book.

I also appreciate the time I was able to spend with Elliott Masie, founder of the Masie Center in Saratoga Springs, New York. Elliott shared with me the latest in learning-related information technology and brainstormed several ideas with me.

I also had extensive electronic mail exchanges with Dave Pollard, chief knowledge officer for Ernst & Young of Canada, and with David Bell, cofounder of The Management Forum for Excellence in Software Development in the United Kingdom. Ithaca College professor Diane Gayeski also shared valuable insights with me via electronic mail and during a visit I made to Ithaca.

I was able to test some of my ideas by holding online seminars, first on the Industry Week forum and later on the Training and Trainers' Forum on CompuServe. My gratitude also extends to audiences for my workshops and presentations to numerous professional and industry groups. Members of those audiences provided me with valuable feedback and suggestions as I formulated some of the approaches I advocate in this book. My students in the graduate management program at Boston's Emmanuel College also provided valuable feedback and, through their questions, forced me to sharpen some of the concepts. The ultimate test of the ideas in this book came from several consulting clients who tried out some of these ideas and, I am happy to report, found them of value.

Finally, I want to thank my wife, Susan, and my daughter, Molly, for their unswerving support for my work on this book, even when it meant changing family plans and schedules.

Introduction

Throughout my career in both business and academia, working in training groups, marketing organizations, and now as a consultant, writer, and speaker, I have focused on adding value not only to the group for which I was working but to the organization as a whole. I always try to keep the larger picture in mind while I do my more focused work. I find that my views and behavior have been unlike those of most of my colleagues in every organization in which I have worked.

Because of the way in which corporate training groups have traditionally evolved, my colleagues are often narrowly focused on their local goals, on working to protect their turf and power. Although they may be successful in their narrow interests, they are not as effective as they could be in contributing to the success of the larger organization. They hoard their knowledge and skills, even when they might solve problems in other parts of the organization. They continuously reinvent the wheel, even when they know it exists elsewhere—often in a better form than they could themselves create.

Are these people so self-centered that they don't care about what happens to the rest of the organization? A few do care, but most respond to the power and organizational structure of which they are a part; they act in self-interest according to how the organization measures their work and rewards their progress, even when they know they could make larger contributions to the organization's success.

I have also been fortunate in being an employee or consultant with several companies and colleges where leaders try hard to break down the barriers to individual and organizational success. These leaders recognize that their organizations can make greater progress if everyone works toward the same goals, rather than having different people pulling in different directions while others resist all attempts at movement in any direction. The organizations fortunate enough to have such leadership create a positive learning environment in which people share their knowledge and skills and strive to achieve not only individual success but also success in meeting larger organizational goals. In these organizations I have found managers who let me experiment with new ways of working, sharing knowledge and skills, and establishing measurements and rewards to support both individual and organizational success.

The Knowledge-Enabled Organization

A common theme in all of these successful institutions—as well as in others I have found in doing research for this book and previous ones—is that they better utilize the knowledge and skills of all employees, regardless of level, function, or location, to meet their goals. Successful companies encourage employee learning, through training programs and, even more so, by enabling and facilitating the exchange of knowledge and ideas and by empowering employees to try new ideas to help improve their own and the company's performance. If a new idea doesn't work out, the employee is rewarded for a thoughtful, well-conceived attempt at improvement—not punished for failing. Managers in these organizations coach employees and reinforce their learning to ensure that new ideas are properly applied to the job to add value to the employee's work.

This is what the knowledge-enabled organization is about. In such an organization, employees acquire the knowledge and skills they need from many different sources, within and without the company. They openly share their own knowledge and skills with others, for they realize that they are all working toward achieving personal and company goals.

I am convinced that only those companies that create a positive learning environment—that encourage learning at all levels and application of that learning to the company's work—will thrive in the future. They spend their time building a better future for themselves and their employees, rather than constantly fighting fires and sacrificing employees to unending financial woes.

In most businesses, when you mention the word *learning*, people immediately think of a formal training group, whether it is called "training and development," "education and training," "employee development," or any of a dozen other titles. Built on a traditional model, these training groups have done more to hinder progress in creating knowledge-enabled organizations than they have helped. A new model is needed, not just for the training group but for the company as a whole. Becoming a knowledge-enabled organization involves not just the training group but everyone from the CEO down; it requires basic changes in how the company is organized and run.

The good news is that you *can* get there from here. This is your guidebook for making the journey.

How This Book Is Organized

In Chapter 1, I indict the traditional model for training and development. The charges fall not only to the training group itself but also to general company management, which has abdicated its own responsibilities for individual and organizational learning and so structured training within the company as to make real learning almost impossible to achieve.

Chapter 2 presents a four-stage learning model and argues that the development of knowledge comes only from applying information and skills to the job to make a positive difference in individual and company results. The model for the knowledge-enabled organization is presented in Chapter 3, along with an inventory of the types of knowledge that individual employees and their companies must develop in order to succeed.

To become a knowledge-enabled organization requires that all learning be tied directly to business goals. Chapter 4 explains how to start with those larger goals and move down to the level of the individual employee, developing for each employee a "learning contract" that specifies the learning needed and how that learning results in achieving personal and organizational goals.

People learn in many ways, not just through formal training programs. In Chapter 5, I examine a wide range of learning options and how they can fulfill employees' learning contracts.

To optimize individual and organization learning, companies must build mechanisms not only for training but also for individuals and groups to share their knowledge with each other. One mechanism for doing this—the knowledge network—is introduced in Chapter 6. For any of these changes to work, the company must build a positive learning environment; this is described in Chapter 7. Although many aspects of organization, policies and procedures, and measurement and reward systems have to change to allow the knowledge-enabled organization to succeed, the changes are most profound for the training group. In Chapter 8, I advise that companies "throw out the training catalog, not the training group." I present a new model for a group I call employee and organizational learning.

Most of the book focuses on how learning takes place within the company. Chapter 10 examines how to move learning activities beyond company boundaries. Finally, in the Afterword, I look at what the future holds for the knowledge-enabled organization.

1

The Great
Training Robbery

Considering all types of training and low levels
of transfer found by HRD researchers, a generous
assumption is that perhaps 50% of all training
content is still being applied a year after training
delivery.

Mary L. Broad and John W. Newstrom
Transfer of Training

According to *Training* Magazine's 1995 annual industry report,
American companies with more than one hundred employees
spent a total of $52.2 billion on training. I believe the great major-
ity of this expenditure was wasted, resulting in no measurable
gains for the companies that invested in this training.

Training groups (I use the term generically to include "training and development," "human resource development," "employee development," and other popular terms) in most
companies today are failures. Not only do they waste millions
of dollars in company funds developing and delivering formal
training programs that create an illusion of progress but few
tangible results, but they also rob their companies and their
companies' employees of real opportunities to succeed.

When the Canadian Imperial Bank of Commerce (CIBC) decided to examine its training efforts, the inquiry took six months
just to determine how much the bank was spending. According

to CIBC's Hubert Saint-Onge, the sum turned out to be "$30 million a year! And one penny out of a hundred hits the mark."

For years, company after company has spent millions of dollars on training, claimed to have "the best trained workforce in the industry," or regularly stated in annual reports that "our people are our most important asset"—only to throw tens of thousands of these well-trained, invaluable assets out on the streets.

Many companies proudly announce that all employees will get one (or two or three) weeks of training per year, or that they spend X percent of payroll on training (typically 5 percent in European countries, but 1.5 percent in the United States). But what does this mean in terms of the company's bottom-line results? Nothing! No specific goal of training *volume* can guarantee that employees will have the knowledge and skills they need to make themselves and their companies successful.

When crunch time comes, and the company needs to reduce headcounts and budgets, training is almost always among the first functions to be hit, and hit hard. Why? Because training groups are generally unable to prove their worth in meeting the challenges of the competitive business environment. Some people in the training field say that this inability stems from poor evaluation methods. I contend that training cannot prove its worth because most of today's training is of little value in terms of meeting company, organizational, and individual goals.

When training is cut back in a company, one often hears a senior executive state that "Training is a luxury we can no longer afford." In this picture, training means sending employees off to expensive, lengthy programs to "reward" them for their hard work, to give them some useful (or not so useful) experiences, a chance to relax, an opportunity to try out some new ideas. These purposes sound reasonable and aren't necessarily "bad." But unless employees can return to their jobs and immediately start applying the content of the training to make a noticeable and positive difference in solving business problems and meeting competitive challenges head-on, then a training program is indeed a luxury that few companies can afford.

Virtually every company with more than one hundred employees does some training. At first, the company may hire an external trainer or consultant to meet some imperative need. For example, as a company grows, employees may be promoted to supervisory positions with no supervisory experience or training; so the company decides to bring in a supervisory training program. Or as the sales force grows, the company decides to do some basic sales training.

As companies grow to a thousand or more employees, they tend to formalize the training role, almost always falling back on the traditional model for training and development. This leads to two sets of problems. First, when the training function is formalized, training becomes the focus rather than *learning*. And second, the traditional model for training and development just doesn't work.

Abdicating Responsibility for Learning

When a company formalizes the training function, it creates a training group and tends to give that group total responsibility for the employees' learning needs. But by placing the focus and responsibility for learning on a training group, company leaders and managers at all levels abdicate their own responsibility for ensuring that employees gain the knowledge and develop the skills they need to succeed as individuals, as functions and departments, and as a company. "That's why we have a training department," the resultant thinking goes, "so managers like me don't have to worry about what our employees need to learn."

This leads to undesirable consequences.

First, no matter how large or how good, a training group cannot hope to understand the company's business as well as the employees and managers do who run the company day in, day out. Without the active advice and participation of line management, the training group can only focus on generic individual skills training. Although worthwhile, that can never address the company's key business requirements and initiatives. By separating training from day-to-day business functions and goals, the company almost guarantees that training programs have little relevance back on the job.

Second, by equating learning with training, the company is

ignoring—not fostering—the daily learning in which all employees must participate if the company is to succeed. Training is an occasional activity; employees might attend a couple of sessions per year. But they must *learn* continuously.

> *By equating training with learning, a company ignores the daily learning in which all employees must participate if the company is to succeed.*

Third, by ceding responsibility for employee learning to the training group, managers ignore their own responsibility to reinforce the integration of learning activities into the fabric of the employee's work. As Chapter 2 discusses, training can only provide employees with information. That information becomes knowledge only if the employee applies it to her job to make a positive difference in both her own work and in the performance of her function or department and the business as a whole. But application of any new skill requires practice and reinforcement. If people gave up on learning to cook the first time they failed, no one would ever learn to cook.

Managers at all levels need to:

* Take responsibility for their employees' learning activities, and their own
* Provide continuous learning opportunities
* Reinforce learning as employees try out new skills

The Company's View of Training Activities

The activity of training is generally viewed as separate from an employee's work activity. Whether employees go off to an in-plant classroom, go away to a training center, or sit at their desks taking a computer-based training program, the time spent on training is generally viewed as time away from the job. This view is promulgated by training professionals, who generally feel that unless they can identify the beginning and ending of a training program, they cannot ask the student to evaluate it.

I believe we need to take a new view of learning activities, whether formal training programs or other methods of learning that I describe later in this book. In this new view, learning is an integral part of each employee's job responsibilities. Even if some time is spent in a formal training program away from the primary job location, this is only a small subset of the learning activities in which every employee must regularly participate.

Because training programs are seen as unproductive time separated from work, many companies view training as an expense. But when learning is understood as central to all work activity, the costs associated with learning activities (including formal training programs) are seen more as an investment than an expense.

The company's view of training and learning is only one part of the problem. There are others inherent in the traditional model for training and development as it has developed in most companies.

The Traditional Model for Training and Development—and Why It Doesn't Work

There is no pure model for training and development. Each company's training efforts have followed their own pattern of growth and adaptation. But a number of patterns and principles provide a good general description of the training and development groups in most companies today. By describing the traditional model, we better understand where it falls short and how the new model of the *knowledge-enabled organization* (which I introduce in Chapter 3) helps overcome the deficiencies of the traditional model.

Examination of the traditional model for training and development is in terms of its:

* Basic model or paradigm
* Goals
* Focus
* Evaluation measures
* Methods

The Basic Model or Paradigm

Traditional training and development groups operate using the academic research model as their basic paradigm. This model places learning theory, instructional design methodologies, and training methods at the forefront, that is, if the programs designed and delivered by the training group meet professional standards and are based on sound learning theory, they must be good.

Because training staff are typically the only people in a corporation who have been trained in such methodology, they are the arbiters of program quality. Therefore, they insist, learning must take place through intentional, trainer-designed, and trainer-directed instructional programs. Programs developed by other groups within the company cannot have the "goodness" of professionally developed and professionally delivered training programs because the people who would do so have not been trained correctly.

> At one time, I worked in a marketing group in a large company that had a well-established, traditional training and development group. In response to an urgent need reported by the salespeople, I developed a short training program on a set of new products. I did so by working with key salespeople, marketing, and product managers. The pilot efforts got rave reviews, and the salespeople who attended the pilot programs reported almost immediate increases in sales of the products covered in the training.
>
> After completing the pilot programs, I went to the formal training group and asked them to take up delivery of the program to a larger sales audience. The training group refused to use the training materials developed for the pilot program.
>
> "We have to follow our standards," the training manager told me. "First, we need to do a needs assessment to find out what the salespeople need to learn. Then we have to learn about the products ourselves and develop learning objectives for the program, design

learning materials, train our instructors on the program, and then do our own pilots. If those go well, we'll put the program materials into production."

"We've already done all that," I replied. "It's all ready to go. All we want you to do is deliver it!"

"But you haven't followed our professional guidelines. We pride ourselves on our professionalism, and we can't just go off and use someone else's materials that don't meet our standards. We have our reputation to think of."

I asked: "If I were to let you take over the project and do it according to your professional standards, when could we get the training out to the sales force?"

"Probably within twelve months," replied the training manager. "Assuming, of course, that you also provide us with the $50,000 we will need to do the project right."

"But the sales force needs the training *now*!" I protested.

"Then you should have come to us a year ago."

"But the products didn't exist a year ago," I said. "They were developed over the past four months."

"That's not my problem."

This myopic view of the training profession's standards of excellence is not uncommon. In fact, this situation follows from one definition of "a professional" as someone who pays more allegiance to the standards of his or her professional field than to the needs of the employer.

There is nothing inherently wrong with the professional standards used by the training profession. Many outstanding training programs have been created using those standards. The point here is that if a corporate training and development group cannot or will not respond to urgent company needs, and if the group refuses to help the company because the company cannot allow sufficient time or resources to create programs according to those professional standards, then the training group is not doing its job, which is to help the company and its employees meet their goals. This is one of the major reasons why corporate training and development groups are increasingly finding themselves in trouble with their companies.

Goals

The major goal of a traditional training and development group is to achieve excellence as measured by the standards of the training profession, that is, by strictly adhering to learning theory and instructional design methodologies. To measure their business, traditional groups typically use such yardsticks as:

* How many students attended programs (headcount or student-days/weeks).
* How much learning was achieved, as measured by pretests and posttests.
* As a result of company pressure, cost per program or per student-week.
* Adherence to professional standards as measured by student surveys, often called "smile sheets." These surveys, usually done at the end of a training program, ask questions such as "Were the objectives clear?" "Did the instructor involve everyone in the class in the discussions?" and "Were the class materials clear?" These are all good questions, but the most important question is almost never asked: "Is this training program going to help you improve your job performance and the company's business results?"

The primary evaluation measure for any training program must be: "Will it help you improve your job performance and the company's business results?"

Politically astute training directors also include in the training group's goals some statement about "supporting the business," but the connections between formal training programs and the company's business goals are tentative at best. In the name of supporting the business, training groups react to requests by business leaders. For example, if the leaders say that the company is going to work toward instituting self-directed work teams or adopting total quality management (TQM) as a philosophy, the training group offers to develop and deliver training related to those initiatives. After all, it is a way of getting more resources for the training department and to "prove" that the training group is responsive to the company's needs.

Too often, the training group insists on large development budgets and long development cycles to develop and deliver programs that meet their professional standards. When this happens, business leaders often hire external consultants and trainers who can deliver more timely and less costly training. The shame of this common occurrence is that it does not upset the training group, which feels that if they can't "do it right"— according to their professional standards—they are better off not doing it at all. Then the same training people wonder why the company's business leaders feel their group is unresponsive to the company's needs.

Focus

The focus of programs developed and delivered by traditional training and development groups tends to be on the individual skills needed to continue business as usual in the company. That is, training tends to reinforce current business practices and to ensure that employees have the skills needed to do the jobs that exist within the company today, and as work is done today. When you see a traditional group working on an innovative program, it is generally because the change has been mandated by company leaders. Traditional training groups most often work in a reactive mode, rather than in a leadership role. Why? Because training groups generally do not understand the company's business and are not involved in planning for the company's future.

Traditional training groups are not active in the company's business planning efforts, so they can only react. They cannot talk the language of the business, but only their own professional jargon, so most new ideas they present to the company's business leaders are rejected. This is not necessarily for lack of merit but because the leaders do not understand what is being proposed and the training group has no credibility since it cannot speak the language of the business.

After the leaders (who find the language of the proposals incomprehensible) reject numerous attempts to help the business through proactive training programs, training groups tend to stop trying. They retreat to their corner and continue doing business as usual.

> Several years ago, I received a call from the training director for a major manufacturing company. He asked me if I would be willing to review the training plan for the company and help the training group translate the plan into language that the company's business leaders would understand and support. I asked him to send me not just the training plan but also the company's annual report, a statement of the top business priorities for the next year, and the sales literature the company gives its customers.
>
> "We really don't have access to that type of material," he told me.
>
> I replied: "If you don't know what business the company is in, how it represents itself to customers, and what the key business strategies are, how can you ever hope to really support the business?"

I see too many mission statements from training groups full of three-dollar buzzwords from the previous year's popular business literature. Few of these have any meaning to the training group or to the company. If training is to succeed in any company, trainers must take the time to learn about the business, learn the vocabulary of the leadership, and translate the business needs into real learning programs integral to the fabric of the company.

Evaluation Measures

The first rule of program evaluation is that evaluation measures should flow directly from the program's goals. The goals of traditional training programs normally are to impart information or develop skills. Using instructional methodologies, pretests and posttests can be devised to measure each student's level of understanding before and at completion of a program, thereby determining how much each student has learned. My experience is that the great majority of corporate training programs do not use pretests and posttests unless they are supporting a competency system.

The only real evaluation measure should be how much of the information and how many of the skills are applied to the job, after the training is completed, to make a positive difference in individual employee performance and in departmental and overall company business performance. Some traditional training groups have started to do surveys of program participants one or three or six months after program completion, but most do no follow up. Worse, few traditional training groups have established any mechanism to reinforce the information and skills imparted in their programs once employees have left the classroom and returned to the job. As Chapter 2 reveals, this practice—or lack of practice—obviates what should be the primary goal of any training effort: knowledge development.

End-of-program participant evaluations (smile sheets) are irrelevant to development of knowledge. These questionnaires focus on the skill of the training group in designing and delivering the program content, not on how much knowledge is developed. A trainer can get perfect ratings on these surveys even when program content is irrelevant to work and makes absolutely no difference in how employees do their jobs.

The American Society for Training and Development (ASTD) is the foremost professional society for corporate trainers. Several years ago, it established a Benchmarking Forum to collect training data that would allow companies to measure how well they were doing comparatively. Its 1995 survey collected data from sixty training organizations in forty-six companies from the United States, Europe, and Australia. Here are the major findings, based on 1995 expenditures and training practices:

* Total training expenditures equaled 2.2 percent of payroll.

* The ratio of training staff members to total employee population was 1 to 186 in companies "that provide a broad range of training services," and 1 to 932 "across all Benchmarking Forum companies."
* The total training expenditure per employee was $1,352.
* Lecture-based delivery represented 69 percent of all delivery time.[1]

Most remarkably, there is not a single measure of how well training programs meet the needs of their businesses.

> There is an old story of a man who is taking a nighttime walk and comes upon two people. They are on their hands and knees under a streetlight, assiduously searching the ground. "What are you looking for?" he asks.
>
> "We dropped the car keys as we were getting into our car," they reply.
>
> Looking around, the man can see no car in the vicinity. "Where's your car?"
>
> "About fifty yards down the road," they answer.
>
> "Then why are you looking here?"
>
> "It's pitch black around the car. The light is much better here."

Most training and development groups face a similar situation. Asked to justify their existence, they focus on the areas where there is light, that is, traditional evaluation measures and questions that are easily answered, such as those in the bulleted list just above. But none of those statistics answer the basic question of how well a training program meets the needs of the business.

Methods

The noted psychologist Abraham Maslow said that if your only tool is a hammer, the whole world looks like a nail. Training and development professionals have been trained on learning theory and instructional methodologies, and so every problem tends to suggest a training solution. Trainers have a wide repertoire of methods, ranging from formal, stand-up lectures to role playing to case studies to self-paced training materials. With the computer revolution have come computer-based, multimedia, and network-based training programs.

Learning theory plays a role in the choice of methods. At other times, cost is the major determinant. For example, one reason why media-based training is becoming so popular is that it can cost less than classroom-based training, especially if travel costs and trainees' time off the job are factored in. With great pressure being applied to training budgets, these cost savings do not go unnoticed by corporate business managers.

Training is not the right solution to every problem. In too many cases, great amounts of money are spent to develop and deliver a training program even when the original problem cannot be solved by training. For example, if plant equipment is worn out and cannot produce products to customer specifications, no amount of training for plant personnel can correct the situation. If a competitor's products or services are clearly superior and less costly, sales training is not the solution. In both cases, a training group asked (and funded) to develop a new training program on quality or sales skills will do so. But no matter how excellent the training program is, how much is invested in the training program, or how long the employees are in a classroom, the problems are not solved.

It is time for training professionals to widen their repertoire to include a wider variety of learning methods. The solutions they propose must be appropriate to the problems being faced and, where learning is the correct solution, more cost-effective.

How Trainers View Their Future

The ASTD spends a lot of time thinking about the future of the training profession. In 1994, the ASTD's board of directors set a study agenda of key trends that would examine "the future needs of the members, the profession, and the society against our year 2000 vision to be a worldwide leader in workplace learning and performance."[2] Among these key trends are:

* The high-performance workplace
* New roles for training
* New technologies for performance
* Management of change

"High-performance workplace" and "high-performance team" have become watchwords for many companies and, therefore, for many corporate training groups. The trainers are very concerned about what skills and knowledge employees need to become "high-performance." Unfortunately, many of the answers they come up with relate to thoroughly traditional programs and training methods. Most trainers don't really understand what a high-performance organization is, or what it takes to become one.

Over the past several years, the training literature has presented many articles and books on how to help your company become a high-performance organization, but very few on how to make the training organization itself high-performance. Most trainers miss the point that becoming a high-performance organization requires the various functions within the company to examine their roles and business processes and to reinvent those processes to better serve the needs of the company and its customers.

This reinvention requires that many functions abandon or modify long-honored standards and methodologies to find a better way of achieving the company's goals. Rather than continuing to view their functions and departments as stand-alone entities, employees are being asked to examine how their work fits into the overall fabric of the company's business. They need not only to focus on maintaining and strengthening their own specialized work but also to work on optimizing the larger business processes of which their work is a part and improving business results. But few trainers are willing to reinvent their own profession and examine their standards and methodologies to determine if they are truly serving the company's goals. Before the training organization can help the company become a high-performance workplace, it must start by reinventing itself.

In most companies, few changes in the training organization or in training delivery methods originate from with the training organization itself. Changes are generally forced by budget cuts, reductions in the number of training employees, or general company reorganizations. There are exceptions. PHH University, part of PHH Corporation, under Director Tim O'Brien, has been training managers to be learning facilitators for more than five years. Blount Industries Canada in Guelph, Ontario, integrates learning of statistical process control (SPC) skills into plant employees' work by using quality department personnel to teach, coach, and reinforce learning as part of the job. But in most companies, new roles are forced on the training group rather than led by the training group. ASTD's concern with "new technologies for performance" reflects both the trend to using computer-based and multimedia training programs and the relatively new arena of "performance support"—an all-inclusive term for technology-based job aids. These topics will be discussed at greater length in Chapter 6, "The Knowledge Network." Regarding the ASTD's key trend of management of change, the board of directors offers a definition: ". . . the management of individual and organizational change in a way that is strategically linked to dynamic changes in global competition—and that supports new performance standards in the workplace. This includes the development of corporate cultures and corporate change methods that enable organizations and individuals to react quickly to the speed and breadth of change in the world today."[3]

What does this definition really mean to the training profession? It has the right words but little content other than to say "we need to pay attention to all of these things, whatever they are." I have seen many mission statements, from corporate training groups in a variety of industries, that are filled with such words. But dig down and you find that on the whole the training professionals in these companies have little idea what the words mean or what they need to do to help their companies change. Even fewer have begun to think about what these changes mean for how they manage the training function within their companies.

Conclusion: The Great Training Robbery

Training programs in most companies today rob the company in two ways. First, because formal training programs developed and delivered by traditional training groups are ineffective in helping the company and its employees succeed in meeting their goals, they waste large amounts of money and time. Second, by creating the illusion that formal training programs can meet the company's learning needs and those of its employees, by separating employees' learning needs and learning activities from their actual work, companies miss opportunities to improve individual and company performance, meet or exceed stated goals, and create real competitive advantage.

To understand the new model of the knowledge-enabled organization, we must start by understanding how people learn and how employees' knowledge and skills can be fostered through a positive learning environment.

Notes

1. Laurie J. Bassi and Scott Cheney, "Changes in Benchmarked Training," *Training & Development*, December 1996, pp. 29–33. Copyright December 1996, the American Society for Training and Development. Reprinted with permission. All rights reserved.
2. "Trends That Will Influence Workplace Learning and Performance in the Next Five Years," *Training & Development*, May 1994. Copyright May 1994, the American Society for Training and Development. Reprinted with permission. All rights reserved.
3. Ibid.

2

Knowledge and Skills: The Keys to Company Success

> In an economy where the only certainty is uncertainty, the one sure source of competitive advantage is knowledge. When markets shift, technologies proliferate, competitors multiply, and products become obsolete almost overnight, successful companies are those that consistently create new knowledge, disseminate it widely throughout the organization, and quickly embody it in new technologies and products.
>
> Ikujiro Nonaka, "The Knowledge-Creating Company," *Harvard Business Review*

Most businesses pay at least some lip service to the idea that the collective knowledge and skills of employees are important to the company's success. Many claim that they foster a learning environment by pointing to large expenditures on training programs and tuition-assistance plans, and by stating in the annual report that "our employees are our most valuable asset." But few companies have made a real commitment to employee and organizational learning, creating an open learning environment, or measuring and rewarding employees based on how much they increase their own knowledge and skills and how much individual knowledge they share with other employees.

The Commitment to Learning: A Case in Point

A true exception to the typical pattern is Buckman Laboratories, a Memphis-based specialty chemicals company with 1,200 employees that does business in eighty countries.

Buckman Labs shows its commitment to education by paying employee tuition for continuing education programs, supporting postsecondary education of the children of all employees, and, in some less-developed countries where high-quality public schools are not prevalent, even helping to pay for private elementary and secondary education of employees' children. Buckman Labs is also committed to ongoing development of all company employees through a wide variety of training programs and less formal learning activities. But what makes Buckman unique is its commitment to the sharing of knowledge among all its employees worldwide. "At Buckman [Labs]," says Buckman Sales Representative Doug Yoder, "when you ask one person a question, you have the power of 1,200 employees behind you—including our CEO, Bob Buckman."

Buckman Labs is in a very competitive industry. Its customers can purchase their chemicals from many sources, not just from Buckman. So why do customers buy from Buckman? The key to their success, according to Chairman Buckman, is knowledge of the customer's business and the ability to respond to customers quickly using that knowledge.

Writing in *The Wall Street Journal*, Jack Falvey said:

> Few managers realize that 80 percent of the sales process is controlled by specific knowledge of a customer's business. Applications experts and industry specialists are secondary to the relationship of trust built by a skilled, professional salesman with his customers. The proper function of a successful sales organization is to provide the sales representative . . . with the goods and services necessary to help his customers do business more effectively.[1]

To accomplish this, employees are measured on being "effectively engaged on the front line." According to the chairman, "Effective engagement is when an associate [employee] takes responsibility for and is actively involved with satisfying the needs and expectations of our customers so that Buckman Laboratories becomes the preferred choice." When he took over the reins of the company from the founder, Stanley Buckman, in the 1970s, he found that only 16 percent of the company's employees were so engaged. Today, that number stands at 50 percent, and the chairman's goal is to reach 80 percent by the year 2000.

A key to achieving Buckman's business goals is effective sharing of the knowledge of all company employees. Bob Buckman views this "as the most difficult aspect of knowledge transfer to achieve. People have taught themselves to hoard knowledge over the years to achieve power. We learned in our school years to acquire and use knowledge, but we did not learn how to share knowledge. Today, we have to reverse that tendency. Today, the most powerful individuals will be those that become a source of knowledge by proactively sharing what they have, or what they can get their hands on, with others."

The ability to solve customer problems comes not just from the training curriculum, but from employees' knowledge of their customers and their customers' businesses. This type of knowledge cannot come from a classroom, but only from real-world experience, from front-line engagement with the customer. It cannot be captured in handbooks or manuals; it exists within the employees' minds. Therefore, it is vital that these knowledge resources be available to help solve problems for all customers. According to Bob Buckman, "Since the bulk of the knowledge of the organization resides in the minds of the associates, we have to allow anybody in the organization to contribute to the solution of the latest problem. You never know where the correct or best answer will come from. In many cases, the best answer will turn out to be the result of the interaction of several minds on the problem."

Knowledge comes from learning. It is crucial to understand this relationship between learning and knowledge before proceeding with a description of mechanisms for transferring and sharing knowledge.

The Four Stages of Learning

Figure 2.1 is a model of how people learn in work situations. The process starts in Stage 1 with data, those myriad bits that float around every company, threatening to inundate us all. In this model, data represent the lowest level of learning. We all know people who carry thousands of bits of data around in their heads but who can never make any use of them, other than repeating them back as trivia.

Management guru Peter Drucker defines information as "data endowed with relevance and purpose."[2] When the individual sees some *relevance* in some data and finds that it has some *purpose* related to the job, the data become information (Stage 2 of the model). This is a filtering process, where we throw all of the data that come our way into a sieve that passes only those bits that are relevant and purposeful. If training programs—traditional or nontraditional—are designed correctly, they focus exclusively on information. A training program filled with data that have neither relevance nor purpose is doubly wasteful—first, in filling employees' heads and files with useless data, and second by wasting the participants' and the company's time, which could have been spent in more relevant and purposeful learning activities.

Filling training programs with extraneous data is only part of the problem. Companies push data at their employees constantly, to the point of data overload. When I worked for Digital Equipment Corporation in the 1980s, I examined how much paper various internal groups sent to the company's salespeople. At that time, the average salesperson received monthly a stack more than two feet high of marketing materials, sales bulletins, technical reports, memos, and other junk mail. And this was from a company that prided itself on early adoption of electronic bulletin boards, notes files, and electronic mail! Not only did this constitute data overload, but it also made it nearly impossible for an individual salesperson to filter out the information that was important to her job and her customers.

Although information is useful, what we want to focus on in all learning activities is development of knowledge. Knowl-

Figure 2.1. The four stages of learning.

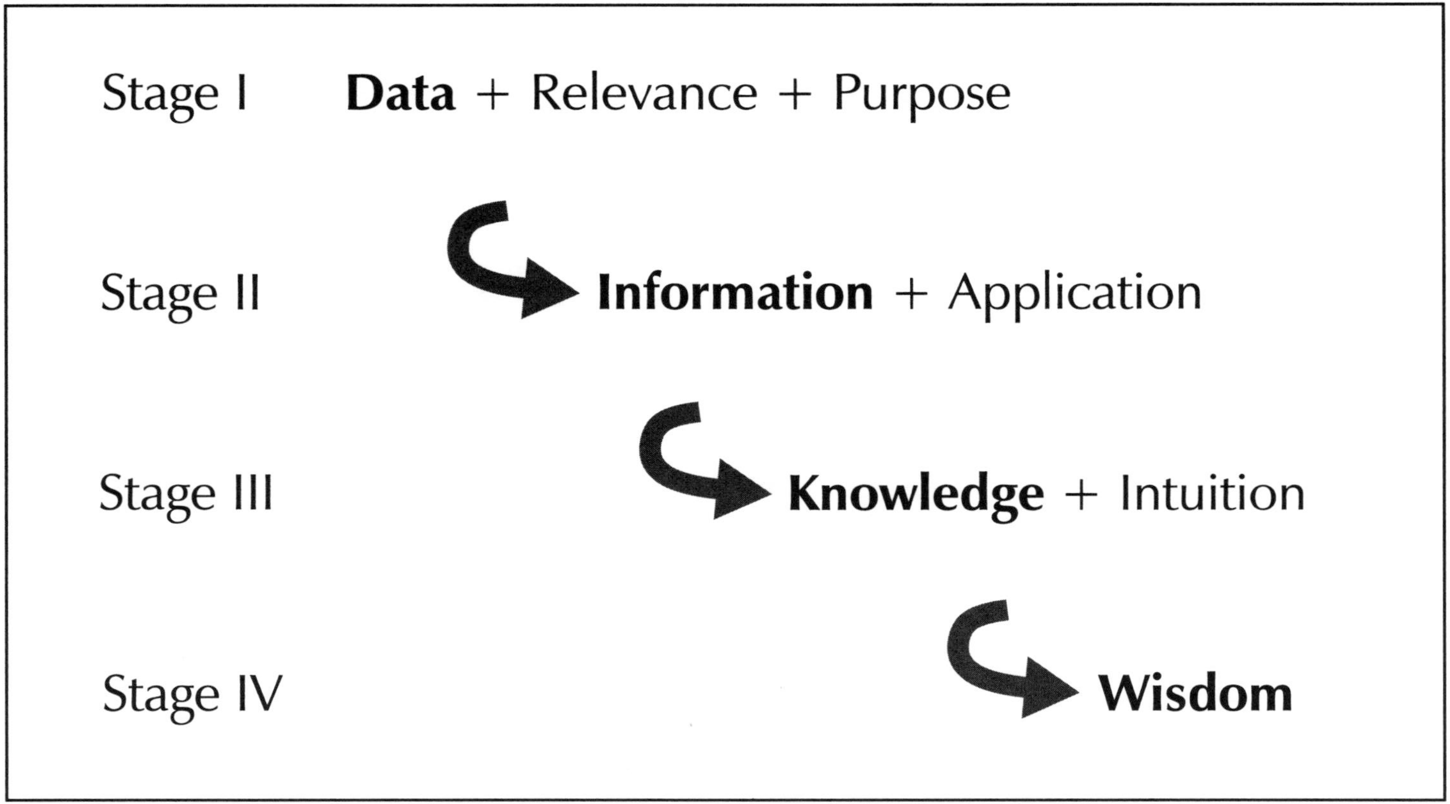

Stage I   **Data** + Relevance + Purpose

Stage II   **Information** + Application

Stage III   **Knowledge** + Intuition

Stage IV   **Wisdom**

edge is developed by taking information and *applying* it to the job (Stage 3). One major problem with most of today's training programs is that much of the information provided is never applied to the participants' work. Unless the information from a training program is applied to the job to make a positive difference in the employee's job performance and in departmental and company business results, there is little purpose to the program. Later in this chapter, we discuss some of the reasons why information from training programs is so rarely applied to the job.

The key to knowledge development is the application of information to the employee's job to make a positive difference in individual and company performance.

The final stage (4) of the model in Figure 2.1 adds to knowledge the *intuition* that comes from experience. The result is wisdom. This intuition is closely akin to what Ikujiro Nonaka and Hirotaka Takeuchi call "tacit knowledge" in their book, *The Knowledge-Creating Company*.[3] This is the knowledge of an operator in a paper plant who "knows" that the mixture in a chemical vat is out of balance because of how static electricity affects his hair as he walks by the vat, or of a detective who "knows" that a suspect isn't telling the full story because of the way she experiences his presence in the room. These usually unconscious thought processes cannot be part of the original learning design because there is little prior understanding of how they are developed. They are usually noticed after the fact. This mixture of knowledge and intuition represents wisdom that cannot really be taught; it must be developed through experience.

> In another old story, a chemical plant came to a complete halt. Something was wrong somewhere in the miles of pipes that threaded through the plant, but no one could find the problem. They exhausted all of their diagnostic tools and the knowledge of every person on the plant staff. Finally, the plant management committee decided it was time to bring in Joe.

Joe had retired two years earlier. In his forty years of working for the company, he had designed this and several other plants and had worked his way up to the position of plant superintendent. There was never a problem that Joe couldn't solve. The current superintendent called Joe, explained the problem, and offered to pay him whatever consulting fee he thought reasonable.

Joe arrived several hours later. He walked through the plant listening to sounds, looking at meters, smelling odors, feeling temperatures. Finally, he stopped at a particular spot and asked one of the plant workers for a hammer. He took the hammer in one hand while feeling along a pipe with his other hand. Finally, he swung the hammer and hit the pipe in a precise spot. Immediately, the plant's systems sprang to life again. Everyone was amazed at Joe's skill.

The next day, the superintendent received Joe's bill. It was for $10,000. He called Joe and said he considered the fee a little out of line for two hours' work (even though the plant shutdown was costing the company more than that each hour). Could Joe provide him with an itemized bill? The bill arrived promptly:

Invoice

Date: _____

To: _____

_____

_____

Item	Description of Service, Parts, etc.	Cost
Item 1:	Hitting pipe with hammer	$1.00
Item 2:	Knowing which pipe to hit and where to hit it	$9,999.00
Please remit within 30 days	*Total*	$10,000.00

Item 2 in the itemized bill represents the tacit knowledge component of wisdom.

How People Learn

People learn in two basic ways. First, they learn from experience, from using their five senses to observe and read, listen, feel, smell, and hear. Sometimes, the learning activity is deliberate, as with attending a class, reading a book, and listening to an audiotape. But people also learn from less deliberate methods. For example, by watching our own manager and other managers, we learn what we like and don't like about particular management styles. (Many people would agree that they have learned more about how to manage people from enduring poor managers than from good ones.)

People also learn from discovery. Sometimes, we employ scientific methods or critical thinking to make new discoveries. Sometimes, our experiences are serendipitous, and we discover things by accident. When we take information from a class or a book and apply it to our jobs, we learn from those experiences and fine-tune solutions to our particular job situations.

But most of all, we learn from other people: listening to people who have knowledge that we would like to develop in ourselves, brainstorming with other individuals who are facing or have faced problems or situations similar to ours, or observing how other people react to and deal with such situations. Because knowledge is developed by application to the job, people are the only repositories of knowledge. Therefore, when we seek knowledge, we must learn from other people.

The ideal learning program is one that, once completed, would guarantee that you learned everything you need to know for the rest of your working and personal life. This, of course, is impossible, for no one can foresee the future. Even two people starting off with similar backgrounds in comparable jobs and career paths will quickly diverge in terms of the knowledge they need, because their experiences, learning styles, and ability to develop and retain knowledge may be quite different.

It is often enough to give people a basic education and enable them to learn as they go. They should learn from their own experiences and from the experiences of others who have gone before them. But in our competitive workplaces, people feel that they either have to know everything or invent solutions themselves. This results in massive duplication of effort, in too frequently providing suboptimal solutions where better solutions already exist, and in wasting large amounts of time and effort trying to train "everyone on everything." The optimal solution is to find the right balance between creating personal knowledge and sharing it.

Sharing Knowledge

Knowledge can only be held by an individual, because for our purposes knowledge comes from applying information to a job. When a person shares his knowledge with another, he is talking from his own experience but can only communicate data. Assuming that the person receiving the shared data sees its relevance to her own job, the data becomes information; but it only becomes her own knowledge as she applies it to her own job.

When we talk about sharing knowledge, or about creating a knowledge database or a knowledge management system, the data within the system or database are just that: data. We call it a "knowledge" system or database because the people who are responsible for placing these data into the system or database must be those with knowledge, that is, those who have created or used the data in their own jobs. As we provide employees with tools and methods of finding the data they need (data relevant to their jobs and for which they have a purpose), we enable those employees to find information. And as employees extract that information and apply it to their own work, it then becomes their personal knowledge (Figure 2.2).

Nonaka and Takeuchi talk about two types of knowledge, explicit and tacit. Explicit knowledge is the easier type to recognize: It "can be articulated in formal language including grammatical statements, mathematical expressions, specifications, manuals, and so forth." Tacit knowledge, on the other hand, "is hard to articulate with formal language. It is personal knowledge embedded in individual experience and involves intangible factors such as personal belief, perspective, and the value system."[4] Tacit knowledge, being closely akin to the intuition and experience components of wisdom in the learning model

Figure 2.2. Sharing knowledge.

Step 1	Knowledge holder sends **data** to knowledge database/system/network
Step 2	Knowledge seeker uses tools to find relevant data **(information)**
Step 3	Knowledge seeker applies information to job to develop **knowledge**
Step 4	As knowledge seeker gains experience and develops intuition, **wisdom** results

of Figure 2.1 and difficult to articulate, cannot be placed in a knowledge database or managed by a knowledge management system. Its communication from holder to recipient must be personal; most often it comes from discussions or demonstrations.

In the story of the malfunctioning chemical plant, the diagnostics and problem-solving procedures used by plant staff represent explicit knowledge. Joe uses tacit knowledge to solve the problem.

Sharing Case Histories at Buckman Laboratories

Michael Charnigo is a group leader for formulator chemicals for Buckman Laboratories. His group of salespeople sell Buckman products to a variety of industries across the United States. In the 1980s, Charnigo recognized that each of his salespeople had unique knowledge of customers' unique applications of Buckman products and services. The question in his mind was how to get these sales representatives to share their knowledge with each other, especially when they rarely met as a group. "I've got a fifty-five-year-old water treatment expert working in one part of the country," Charnigo said. "How do I transfer his knowledge to a new thirty-year-old representative in another part of the country?"

Early on, Charnigo experimented with asking each of his people to write one unique case history and share it with the other representatives. The case history would be about how a customer developed a unique application of a Buckman product, an application not suggested in the product specifications, manuals, or training programs. Almost immediately, new sales resulted. "One of my people wrote about how a canner in California's Imperial Valley was using a certain Buckman product in canning tomato products. My person in Texas saw that application story and decided to visit a canning factory in his area—a potential customer he had never called on." The case history and subsequent sales call resulted in a substantial new sale of the product and opened the door to selling other Buckman products to the Texas canning plant.

The stories of unique applications would never have been made known to other sales reps without the case history exercise. But the case histories were only a start to Buckman's efforts to develop and share new knowledge. As we see in Chapter 6, Buckman Laboratories has greatly improved on this one-time case history effort through development of a unique knowledge network.

Barriers to Knowledge Development

We can use the model of the four stages of learning (Figure 2.1) to examine some common barriers to knowledge development:

* Unavailability of data
* Inability to find relevant, purposeful data
* Failure to apply information to the employee's work
* Failure to recognize and share tacit knowledge

Unavailability of Data

In Stage 1, people starting the learning process have to gain access to the data they need. If these data don't exist or aren't accessible, no learning can take place. Sometimes, this happens because a problem is new and there aren't any data relating to it, but more often the people who have the data just don't make them available. Why?

People carry a lot of data in their brains without realizing the data might have value to other people. For example, early in your career you worked for company X. You may not know that your current employer is trying to sell a product or service to company X and might value your earlier experience there in deciding how to sell to them. In the Buckman Labs example, you might not know that the solution you sold to your customer has value to other customers in the same industry or in a different one. If you don't think about the larger context of the company's business, or if you don't believe your experience is valuable to other employees, you will never bother to make the relevant data available. This individual myopia can keep data from ever being shared with others who might find them of great value.

Just as you can bar others from learning because of a myopic view of your own knowledge, so can your department or function be guilty of what I call functional myopia. When a function or department is so focused on its local goals that it never shares its knowledge with other groups in the company, a lot of data can be lost. By playing the cards close to the chest, functions and departments often force other groups to live with suboptimal solutions, reinvent solutions that already exist, leave problems unsolved, and let opportunities go by the board.

For example, a manufacturing department doesn't share information on a new manufacturing technique with a design engineering group because it views the technique as one to be used solely to reduce manufacturing costs. What the manufacturing department doesn't realize is that if the design engineers knew of the new technique, it might help reduce design costs as well, resulting in even greater savings to the company. One of the primary reasons why so many of the popular transformation programs of the 1990s place a strong emphasis on cross-functional collaboration is to overcome this barrier.

Company culture can also act as a barrier to sharing data. If, for example, a company's culture promotes a competitive, winner-take-all mentality, employees hoard their data to give them an edge in beating out other employees for rewards. Many companies also suffer from a "not invented here" mentality, believing that they must find all solutions internally. Companies with this type of myopia do not allow employees to seek data outside the company to help solve company problems. They don't develop libraries of external materials, give employees access to external databases, or allow employees to benchmark against other companies.

Inability to Find Relevant, Purposeful Data

Even if relevant data exist, these data may be useless unless employees have a method of finding what they need. There are two major barriers to attaining Stage 2 of the learning model.

First, many companies accumulate massive amounts of data that reside in a wide array of computer databases and applications throughout the company. But few companies find or develop effective tools and processes to make data available to all employees. Because of these labyrinths, employees seeking data relevant to their jobs either don't know that the relevant data exist or have no way to access the data they know of.

The second barrier to Stage 2 learning results from managers who do not value learning, who feel that employees searching out others' knowledge are wasting time and should focus on getting their "real work" done. How many managers, in any functional area of your company, would give high marks to an employee who asks to spend one day a month at the local university library reviewing the latest trade and professional journals? Most managers would tell him to do it on his own time and use company time for "productive" activities.

Failure to Apply Information to the Employee's Work

Even when an employee finds information that can add value to her job, she may be barred from applying it to her work, from transforming the information into personal knowledge. Why? There are several common reasons.

You attend a training program that really changes your view of your work. But when you return to your job, find that although you have changed, the company and your job haven't. You are faced with the pressures of catching up following your absence to attend the program, so the new ideas that you really intend to implement lose out to the day-to-day pressures from the job.

If we want employees to transform the information they have gathered into knowledge, if we want them to make a real difference in how work is done, we have to provide employees with the opportunity to try out those new ideas and master new skills. Too often, we never allot the time.

As employees gather new information from any source, they often don't know what questions to ask. They cannot foresee the problems that inevitably arise when they try to apply their new skills to the job. And when they do try to integrate their new learning with their jobs, they almost never have any way of asking questions or getting coaching or reinforcement. The instructors in the training program are back in the classroom teaching the subject matter to other students. The authors of the books or articles are unavailable. Other employees who shared their knowledge with them are busy with their own jobs. The employees' managers, never having attended the program or read the materials, are of little help. So when employees try out their new ideas and come face-to-face with inevitable problems, they abandon the new ways in favor of the old, inefficient solutions that still get the job done.

Managers also obstruct applying information by not allowing employees to try out new ideas. "That may work in the classroom," they say, "but this is the real world. We've been doing the same work here with the same old methods for years, and we always make our numbers. Don't make waves." How many times can you hear this message before you refuse to consider anything new?

Failure to Recognize and Share Tacit Knowledge

Tacit knowledge is very difficult to put into a database or a training program. Because it is based on experience in applying knowledge and intuition built on that experience, it cannot be easily presented in a written form but instead must be shared via discussion or demonstration. While many managers recognize that some of their people develop reputations as "magicians," "wizards," or "gurus," and they value these people for their expertise, few are willing to free these valuable resources for such sharing activities. Rather, they hide these resources from others in the company, fearing that someone else will try to steal them away. They discourage these people from taking time from their work to hold discussions or do demonstrations, not only in person but even electronically.

If the company wants to enable other employees to develop similar wisdom, the only way is through sharing. This is a major reason why the current movement to media-based and network-based individualized instruction is not going to yield the same harvest of knowledge that traditional face-to-face instruction can: Students cannot benefit from the wisdom of the expert or the guru's tacit knowledge through the use of such media.

People who hold tacit knowledge are also unwilling to share it with others if sharing poses a threat to the individual's job security. As thousands of companies continue to downsize, people holding tacit knowledge know that their stock of wisdom provides some advantage over other employees who don't have as much. Facing the downsizing ax, employees hoard their wisdom to provide some measure of job security. As Brooke Manville and Nathaniel Foote of McKinsey & Co. put it: "Who wants to share what they know when the boss is looking to cut headcount and consolidate expertise in a smaller and cheaper organization?"[5]

Conclusion: Creating a Positive Learning Environment

From a company perspective, the key to creating knowledge and skills that support its goals is creating a positive learning environment where:

* All employees recognize the need for continuous learning to improve their own performance and that of the company overall.
* The company develops a culture that facilitates and encourages learning and open sharing of knowledge and ideas.
* The company provides the opportunities and means for a wide variety of learning activities, sharing of knowledge and ideas, and coaching and reinforcement of newly acquired knowledge and skills.

Many companies have deluded themselves into believing that they have done all this. They point to large investments in training programs, establishment of companywide communications and information networks, and company mission statements that stress how important employees are. Unfortunately, many of these companies still have poor learning environments because of the barriers mentioned in this chapter, and because of other inhibitors: misdirected measurement and reward strategies, rigid organizational structures, and policies and procedures that force people to work in the same old ways even while the leaders are pointing to new directions. It's the old story of the emperor's new clothes; the emperor is convinced that the company is moving in the right direction, but everyone else sees right through the situation.

In Chapter 3, we examine just what it means to be a knowledge-enabled organization. We see in the experiences of a variety of businesses the benefits of creating a positive learning environment where knowledge and skills become key enablers of the company's success.

Notes

1. Jack Falvey, "Big Blue on the Comeback Trail," *Wall Street Journal,* July 12, 1993, p. A12.
2. "The Coming of the New Organization," *Harvard Business Review,* January–February 1988, p. 46.
3. Oxford, 1995.
4. Ibid., p. viii.
5. Brooke Manville and Nathaniel Foote, "Strategy as If Knowledge Mattered," *Fast Company,* May–June 1996.

3

The Knowledge-Enabled Organization

[K]nowledge is action. Knowledge is focused innovation. Knowledge is all-hands contribution. Knowledge is the pooled expertise and efforts of networks and alliances. Knowledge is value-adding behavior and activities. The upshot is that knowledge differentiates products and services from those of other providers. Knowledge, therefore, transforms organizational processes and outcomes—and thus transforms organizations themselves.

Professor Oren Harari, "The Brain-Based Organization," *Management Review*

When a company learns to utilize and foster the growth of the knowledge and skills of all employees across all functions and levels, integrate learning activities into every employee's work, encourage and reinforce all modes of learning, and align all of this learning with the company's strategic business directions, it becomes a knowledge-enabled organization. The knowledge-enabled organization meets or exceeds its goals, for the company as a whole and for the individual employee.

This is important for companies in all industries, not just those that would appear to be "knowledge-based." Whether you are in a service or a manufacturing industry; whether you are selling knowledge, sophisticated technical products, or commodity products and services; the knowledge and skills of your employees are what really differentiate you from your competitors.

The knowledge and skills of your employees are what really differentiate you from your competitors.

Ernst & Young, a "big six" accounting and consulting firm, sells the knowledge and skills of its employees. It has no other product. Recognizing the need to capitalize on the massive knowledge stores in its thousands of employees worldwide, the company has established the position of chief knowledge officer (CKO) in its businesses in major countries. The CKO builds the company's stocks of individual and organizational knowledge and enables employees to locate and access the knowledge and skills they need to meet customer requirements.

Another international accounting and consulting firm, Andersen Worldwide, has developed an electronic system, ANet, to link its 82,000 employees in 360 offices in seventy-six countries to tap "into otherwise dormant capabilities and [to expand] the energies and solution sets available to customers."[1] Similar efforts are well under way in all the major international consulting firms.

Xerox Business Systems (XBS) provides copying, mailroom, and other commodity business services to customers on an outsourcing basis. When you have a business that, like XBS, is growing 40 percent a year, more than half of your current employees have been with the company for less than two years. According to Chris Turner of XBS, "When you're growing this fast, the most important issue you have to contend with is organizational knowledge."[2] XBS is on its way to becoming a knowledge-enabled organization, with its basic strategy being "[to create] an organization of 15,000 effective businesspeople, where everybody thinks about the future, everybody amazes customers, everybody manages the bottom line."[3]

But XBS is selling low-cost commodity products and services, not high-priced accounting, audit, and consulting services as does Ernst & Young. How can knowledge play such an important role in the company's success? Turner says the arguments for turning XBS into a knowledge-enabled organization are simple:

> Think about it. There are other companies in the outsourcing business who can offer equipment, supplies, and people. Our only differentiator is the kind of community we are. It comes down to three questions: If you were a customer, who would you rather work with— someone who's doing business like it was done fifteen years ago, or someone who's using cutting-edge thinking? If you were a talented person looking for a job, where would you rather work? And if you were president of the company, would you rather try to achieve success with a small group of top managers doing all the thinking, or with all 15,000 people contributing to the business?[4]

A similar argument is made by Buckman Laboratories. As a customer of the chemical manufacturer, would you rather depend on the knowledge and skill of a single local salesperson or have access to the combined knowledge and skills of all twelve hundred Buckman employees?

Knowledge-Based Manufacturing

In its annual competition naming "America's Best Plants," *Industry Week* has focused on finding quantum-level improvements in manufacturing results. It is clear from the stories of the plants selected as among America's best that virtually every strategy and program that distinguishes them from the run of the mill is knowledge-based. Gone are the times when a central planning staff made all decisions, where workers were just another factor of production expected to do their jobs and not think. The key to success for every one of these plants was to broaden the knowledge base: to involve every employee in understanding and helping meet company goals; use the knowledge and ideas of all employees, not just planners and managers; and have everyone in the plant develop more knowledge about customers and the manufacturing and business processes, and apply that knowledge to improve manufacturing processes.

At Honeywell's Industrial Automation & Control plant in Phoenix, this involved making significant improvements in quality, cycle time, and materials management across the entire manufacturing process. According to Gale Kristof, the plant's manager of worldwide manufacturing programs, "Aggressive goals were intentionally selected to cause all areas to rethink how they did business rather than just modify the existing methodology."[5] Each improvement came from developing more widespread knowledge of the manufacturing process and then applying the knowledge and skills of all plant employees, at all levels, to bettering cycle time and utilization of space and equipment.

At Northrop Grumman Corp.'s Naval Systems Plant in Cleveland, knowledge-based improvement efforts included just-in-time (JIT) manufacturing, focused factories, work cells, and a demand-based pull system. Process mapping to understand how the plant really worked was a key step. "The results: a 70% reduction in overall process steps and cycle-time reductions of 75%."[6]

At the Asea Brown Boveri (ABB) Industrial Systems plant in Columbus, Ohio, workers have been given control of their own work. According to Teri Bahnick, a twelve-year veteran of the plant, "once [you're] equipped with the process knowledge, having broad decision-making responsibility assures quality, facilitates work flow, and enhances job satisfaction and self-esteem."[7] George Morris, the plant's vice-president of manufacturing and supply management, states that the organization's intent is to "create a caring, learning environment where all teams think, act, and participate as owners in a successful, ongoing business."[8]

These are all examples of how successful companies rely on the knowledge and skills of their employees to achieve excellence. Lawrence Prusak, of Ernst & Young's Center for Business Innovation, states:

> Those of us who are attempting to do research in the areas of sustainable competitive advantage have come to the conclusion that the only thing that gives an organization a competitive edge—the only thing that is sustainable—is what it knows, how it uses what it knows, and how fast it can know something new.[9]

A company's knowledge and skill requirements can be understood first in terms of individual employees and second in terms of collective organizational knowledge.

Knowledge Requirements: Individual Employees

To become a knowledge-enabled organization, a company's employees must develop three types of knowledge:

1. Knowledge about the company
2. Knowledge about customers
3. Knowledge about the company's business processes

Knowledge About the Company

All employees, regardless of level or function, must understand the company for which they work. They need to know what business the company is in. In today's corporation, many employees have such a myopic view of their work that they have little idea what the company as a whole does, that is, the company's mission, its vision of the future, and its near-term and long-term goals, as well as knowledge of the company's products and services—what the company sells to its customers.

> "I didn't realize how hard it was to get people to understand what we are trying to do here," says John

Haleda, former CEO of Wynn's Climate Systems in Fort Worth. "Now I realize they don't have my experience, contacts, and information. No wonder they didn't grasp it all easily. Shame on me for not understanding their perspective."[10]

Employees also need to develop a basic understanding of the company's financial statements, what they mean, how the company derives its profit, what the company's major costs are, etc. Republic Engineered Steels CEO Russell W. Meier has seen a great improvement in the company's bottom line from regularly sharing economic data with employees. The result, he says, is that "everyone can give information to improve their area of the business. No system is perfect, but on balance Republic has workers with a better broad-based understanding of the economics of the company and the pressure we face every day in the marketplace."[11]

Employees need to understand how the company is organized and where they, as business units, functions, departments, and individuals, fit into that organization. This knowledge enables employees to see the larger picture, have some idea of where to go with ideas, seek help with problems, and find opportunities for new business that cross traditional group boundaries.

I once attended a national conference at MIT. In talking with some other attendees, I heard about several problems they were having in dealing with my company. Although the problem areas had nothing to do with my own work in the company, I took responsibility for following up to see if I could get the problems solved. Through my knowledge of the organization, and the informal network I had developed within the company over the years, I was able to get the right people working on each of the problems; eventually, the problems were all solved.

The solutions were not unique, nor was access to the right organizations and people limited to those at my level. But the field-based company employees who dealt with these customers daily did not know about the resources or how to locate them. Without knowledge of existing solutions and where to find them, these customers' problems remained unsolved.

Knowledge About Customers

Every employee must develop knowledge about customers, who they are, why they do business with the company, and what they are seeking. What is the basis for the company's success (or failure): cost? quality? availability? service?

Every employee must view her job as serving customer needs. Whether she has direct contact with customers or is buried in a support or service function, she must realize that without customers there would be no paychecks. Whenever she answers a telephone, she may have direct customer contact, even if it is a wrong number.

> Have you ever reached a wrong number in the company you were calling? Did the person who answered just tell you that you had the wrong number and hang up? Or did he take the time to find out who you were trying to call and get you connected to the right person? How would you, as a customer, feel about the company in both instances?

One business that has a very clear focus on its customers is EMC Corp. of Hopkinton, Massachusetts. This dedication to listening to customers starts with CEO Michael Ruettgers, who makes it abundantly clear that his entire focus is on customers. It is further explained by the director of industry marketing, John Hart: "We want to have a sound understanding of the traits, needs, and hot buttons of our customers," whether they are in financial services, telecommunications, retail, manufacturing, or health care. "That feedback lets us become a consultant to the customer so they will come to us with ideas on product direction and product services that can put more space between us and our competition."[12]

If employees are not customer-focused, if they do not know

how the company obtains and retains customers, they cannot work toward meeting customer requirements. They may end up designing and building new products that are too technically sophisticated, expensive, or unreliable to satisfy customers. Without knowledge of customers and the company's customer strategies, employees cannot align their own work to support those strategies.

The director of R&D at one medical chemical company requires his scientists to work regularly with their customers. Not only does this give them a better idea of what the customer needs, it also lets them bask in the customer's appreciation when they deliver a product they created at the customer's request.[13]

Knowledge About the Company's Business Processes

No matter how a company is organized, it has a set of key business processes through which it gets its work done. There may be an engineering-manufacturing-marketing process, a sales process, a billing process, etc. Every employee in the company must develop a basic understanding of the major business processes and a more detailed understanding of the business process of which his job is a part.

Process mapping helps individuals, teams, departments, and business units understand how their own work contributes to the larger work of the company. Without process knowledge, individuals often become so focused on optimizing their own piece of the puzzle that they sometimes adversely affect other parts of the process. As consultant Steve Patterson says, without such process understanding employees' "common agenda and mutual purpose [can become] 'lost in translation'." He continues:

> This problem can be solved by modeling the core work of a business in a unique, standardized vocabulary that transcends function and discipline boundaries. This modeling provides a common context, a shared understanding of the work of the business and of the roles that each function and discipline play in doing that work. It provides the means to establish a common set

of beliefs and definitions that drive the business as a whole.[14]

Just-In-Time, Just Enough Knowledge

Knowledge requirements differ for each employee. Referring back to the learning model presented in Chapter 2, we recall that knowledge is developed when an employee takes information relevant to her job and applies it to her work. Certainly there is some basic level of information about the company, customers, and business processes that all employees need. Beyond that basic level, knowledge development must be tailored to the needs of each employee, of each job within the company. To try to give all information to all employees only results in information overload, where so much information is being transmitted that employees cannot sort out which pieces are important, and thus they ignore all of it.

Knowledge development must be tailored to the needs of each employee and of each job within the company, using just-in-time learning along with just enough learning methods.

The concept of just-in-time (JIT), which was originally developed in the manufacturing arena, can provide useful guidance here. With JIT manufacturing, materials and parts are ordered and delivered just as they are needed in the manufacturing process. We need to move learning activities to this same plane of performance, so that employees can access the information they need at the time they need it. And the amount of information they receive should match their need. If an employee needs to learn how the results of his work are used, he shouldn't have to learn all the details of the entire manufacturing process. Often, it is enough for each employee to learn about how his work relates to his supplier (that is, the person from whom he gets his work) and his customer (the person to whom he sends his completed work).

For example, a person who enters billing data into a system

doesn't need to know the computer code used to develop the system or how the salesperson won the sale reflected in the invoice. But it may help to know how the data being entered is used by the accounts receivable department. Developing just-in-time, just enough learning activities is not a trivial exercise. Chapter 8 offers methods for developing these types of learning opportunities.

Skill Requirements: Individual Employees

Along with these basic knowledge requirements, employees also need to develop the skills they need to do their jobs. In the old, bureaucratic, mechanistic models of the corporation, these skill requirements were very narrowly defined. For the twenty-first-century organization, we require a broader definition of skill requirements, starting with a set of generic business skills needed by all employees:

* Communications skills
* Mathematics skills
* Self-management skills
* Business skills
* Team skills
* Function-specific skills

Communications Skills

No employee today works in total isolation. As we evolve toward more integrated work places, placing greater emphasis on high performance work teams, communications skills are ever more important. How many good ideas are lost in your company every day because someone with an idea is not confident that he can express it clearly? Rather than embarrass himself because of poor written or oral communications skills, he keeps his mouth shut and doesn't share his ideas. Steve Kerr, General Electric's chief learning officer (CLO), puts it this way:

The acid test I use when I teach managers is to say, "I'll bet every one of you goes home at night with stuff in your head that would help the company. You know how to make the company more effective and you don't tell. I'll bet every one of you goes home at night with stuff in your head that would help your boss do a better job, but you don't tell him or her because it's awkward or risky. Imagine if you could just unleash the power of the collective knowledge right in this room; imagine the good it would do."[15]

Certainly, lack of effective communication skills is not the only reason why people don't communicate their ideas. Other reasons, discussed elsewhere in this book, are a perceived need to hoard knowledge, managers who don't value employee's ideas, the not-invented-here syndrome, and so on.

But if your company wants to create an open learning environment, where employees regularly share their knowledge and skills with each other, then all employees must have basic communication skills, in listening, reading and writing, and presentation.

Mathematics Skills

Every employee needs to master basic math skills, at least to the level of algebra. In today's world of statistical process control charts and spreadsheets, elementary understanding of algebra and statistics is mandatory for all employees. If we want employees to understand the company's balance sheets and income statements, so as to find new ways of reducing costs and improving financial results, then no employee can be deficient in these skills.

Self-Management Skills

Few companies today, if any, can guarantee lifetime employment. Employees must take responsibility for planning and managing their own careers, their own learning, and how they apply that learning to their jobs. In the 1970s, when the first large layoffs were taking place in the computer industry in companies such as Prime Computer (which no longer exists) and Wang Laboratories (currently a shadow of its former self), an article in *The Wall Street Journal* posed the question: When a company lays off a third of its workforce, are you better off being in the group that has departed or the group that is left? The quandary has repeated itself countless times in virtually every industry: The people left behind become so paranoid about who will be the next to face the ax that they lose their focus on their work. If we are to avoid these situations, employees must learn how to manage themselves and their careers so that although they may not have a guarantee of lifetime employment, they can have reasonable assurance of lifetime employability.

So what skills do employees need? They need skills to manage their own lives and their own careers. As Chapter 4 shows, they also need skills to manage their own job performance and their own learning. The company's role is not that of a parent but of a learning facilitator, making learning opportunities available to employees and providing pointers and access to the necessary learning resources within and without the company.

It also behooves the company to teach employees how to learn. As the next several chapters demonstrate, the traditional model for corporate training and development has made the employee dependent upon the training organization, that is, when faced with a learning need the employee asks: "Where's the course? Where do I sign up? Teach me!" In the knowledge-enabled organization, employees must take responsibility for their own learning. But this can happen only when the employee knows how to learn, where to find appropriate learning resources, and how to contract for the learning needed.

Business Skills

As already mentioned, all employees must learn to understand the company's basic business processes and its financial statements. Also within this category of business skills fall problem-solving and decision-making skills, also known as critical-thinking skills. Employees need to learn how to question basic assumptions, consider alternatives, and make wise decisions. As we push decision-making responsibility closer and closer to the customer, we cannot expect employees who have spent their lives implementing decisions their managers have made to know automatically how to analyze problems and make their own decisions. This is a skill set that must be learned by employees at every level of the company.

Team Skills

The high-performance work team, aka the self-managed work team, has become a mainstay of almost every popular corporate transformation program of the past twenty years. But teamwork is not the "natural" way for people to work. For most of our lives, beginning at the earliest age, we are taught the importance of individual achievement. In most of our school experiences, *teamwork* was another term for *cheating*.

Many companies have followed what I call (with apologies to George Eastman) the Kodak approach to teamwork: Throw a group of people into a dark room and see what develops. Over and over again, companies have had disastrous results from reducing headcount by announcing to a work group that they will no longer have a manager and telling them to go ahead and manage themselves. Without basic team skills, as well as the other requisite skills discussed in this chapter, effective teamwork just isn't going to happen. People need to learn how to work as part of a team.

Function-Specific Skills

In addition to generic skills, an employee has to acquire the skills needed to do her specific job. Whether in accounting, inventory, engineering, or sales, there is a set of function-specific competencies each employee must achieve to get the job done. Too often, companies focus solely on the function-specific skills and disregard the generic skills we have just discussed. This may lead to functional excellence, but it almost always results in suboptimization of the company's overall business goals.

Organizational Knowledge

Ideally, the organization's knowledge would be the sum of the knowledge and skills of its employees. But not all employee knowledge and skills can be captured by the organization. Explicit knowledge—knowledge that can be represented as data and placed in manuals and databases—can certainly be captured, but it rarely is. This is knowledge about company products and services; the company's organization and business processes; customers and suppliers; the company's patents, trademarks, service marks, and licenses for various types of technologies and processes, etc. All of these types of knowledge constitute the company's "intellectual assets."

Tracking Intellectual Assets at Dow Chemical

One company that has seriously attempted to take stock of its intellectual assets is Dow Chemical. Dow's efforts began with its patents. Over the years, Dow had accumulated an ever-growing portfolio of nearly thirty thousand patents. According to Dow's global director of intellectual asset and capital management, Gordon Petrash, "Nothing ever left, and we just kept piling them on. It made it hard to aggressively license our technology."[16] As reported in the *Journal of Business Strategy*: "The problem was compounded by the fact that whatever knowledge existed regarding what was in the stuffed patent files could be found only in the research and manufacturing departments. The business staff was completely in the dark."[17]

Aside from being inaccessible, the information on the patents could not be classified as "knowledge" because it wasn't being applied to work. The patents were therefore not assets, but rather liabilities because they entailed upkeep and maintenance costs with few benefits to the company. The patent information (as well as information on trademarks, copyrights, and processes owned by Dow) didn't become company knowledge until it was first placed in a database and then Petrash organized teams to determine which of the assets held value for the company and which did not.

Along with these documents, Petrash asked the teams to identify "key technology know-how" within the company: the R&D and manufacturing processes that were unique to the company and that added value to Dow's business and gave the company a competitive advantage. According to Petrash, "The teams are asking what information is key, where it resides, and how it's articulated. They are finding out who keeps what knowledge and what the associated patents are. They're figuring out where knowledge fits into the process. They're setting parameters."[18]

The point here is that these types of data can have value to the organization only if they are organized so that the people who need them can access them to improve their own, their group's, and the company's performance in meeting business goals.

Tacit knowledge, including employee skills, is not so easily represented and therefore cannot be captured. About the best a company can do with tacit knowledge is to create an environment where all employees are encouraged to share their tacit knowledge with others. (It would be better yet if their sharing were measured and rewarded.) According to Dave Pollard, chief knowledge officer of Ernst & Young of Canada, "You can capture knowledge about skills in an inventory, but you cannot capture the skills themselves."[19]

Companies can also create networks of people who have such knowledge, facilitating the job of finding the knowledge and skills that an employee may need at any given time. Harris Corp. of Melbourne, Florida, for example, "is concentrating more on disseminating information and building a network of workers and information technology to support this effort. Rather than keying on teams, Harris appoints individuals as 'certified practice experts' in various areas." This closely follows the model used by Ernst & Young of Canada. Pollard points out, "What E&Y calls a 'Knowledge Network' is the team of people (internal and external) who share knowledge and expertise in a particular subject area."

We examine more closely how companies can build and use their knowledge networks and databases in Chapter 6.

Conclusion: The Knowledge-Based Organization

The knowledge-enabled organization is one in which:

* The company recognizes that the collective knowledge and skills of its employees provide the company's only source of sustainable competitive advantage.
* The company uses the knowledge and skills of all employees, regardless of level, function, or location, to help meet individual, functional, department, and overall company goals.
* Every employee has the means to locate the knowledge and skills of other employees to improve individual and company performance.
* The company provides just-in-time, just enough learning opportunities to all employees to enable them to gain the knowledge and skills needed to do their jobs.
* The company builds a culture that nurtures a positive learning environment.

In the knowledge-enabled organization, continuous improvement means continuous learning. The next chapter shows how today's leading companies have discovered that learning is what matters, and that learning encompasses much more than formal training programs.

Notes

1. James B. Quinn, Philip Anderson, and Sydney Finkelstein, "Managing Professional Intellect: Making the Most of the Best," *Harvard Business Review*, March–April 1996, p. 76.
2. Chris Turner, as quoted by Alan Webber in "XBS Learns to Grow" in the October–November 1996 issue of *FAST COMPANY* magazine, p. 113. c 1996 by *FAST COMPANY*. All rights reserved. For U.S. subscriptions, call: 800/688-1545. Outside the U.S., call: 303/604-1465.
3. Ibid., p. 115.

4. Ibid.
5. Theodore Kinni, "America's Best Plants," *Industry Week* (Compu-Serve online edition), October 7, 1996.
6. Ibid.
7. Ibid.
8. Ibid.
9. Lawrence Prusak, "The Knowledge Advantage," *Strategy & Leadership*, March–April 1996, pp. 6–8.
10. Mark A. Frohman, "Unleash Urgency and Action," *Industry Week* (CompuServe online edition), November 4, 1996.
11. Scott Robertson, "Meier: Education, Communication Seen as Key," *American Metal Market*, September 27, 1995, p. 7.
12. Ibid., p. 7.
13. Frohman, op. cit.
14. Steve Patterson, "Returning to Babel," *Management Review*, June 1994, pp. 44–46. Reprinted by permission of the publisher, copyright 1994. American Management Association, New York. All rights reserved.
15. Richard M. Hodgetts, "A Conversation With Steve Kerr," *Organizational Dynamics*, Spring 1996, pp. 68–79. Reprinted by permission of the publisher, copyright 1996. American Management Association, New York. All rights reserved.
16. Rick Mullin, "Knowledge Management: A Cultural Evolution," Journal of Business Strategy, September–October 1996, pp. 56–59.
17. Ibid.
18. Ibid.
19. Pollard is quoted from personal interviews and electronic mail exchanges.

4

The Learning Contract: Tying Learning to Business Goals

Our plans miscarry because they have no aim. When a man does not know what harbor he is making for, no wind is the right wind.

Seneca (4 B.C.–A.D. 65)

One key to creating a knowledge-enabled organization is the practice of developing individual employee learning contracts for every employee in the company. The learning contract specifies the knowledge and skills that the employee must acquire over the next year to meet individual goals. These goals are tied directly to functional, departmental, and business unit goals and must have a direct relation to the company's overall business goals.

The learning contract is more than the typical section on employee development found in many employee evaluation forms. In the knowledge-enabled organization, the learning contract is the principal guide for learning activities to be undertaken by the employee. The learning contract specifies not only the learning that the employee must pursue, but also how the employee's learning is transferred back to the job and the changes in business results that are expected once the transfer is complete. In the knowledge-enabled organization, fulfillment of the learning contract is one of the primary measures used in the employee's performance and salary evaluations. It is what makes the employee accountable.

The learning contract specifies not only the learning that the employee must pursue, but also how that learning is transferred back to the job and the changes in business results expected once the transfer is complete.

Hubert Saint-Onge, of the Canadian Imperial Bank of Commerce (CIBC) in Toronto, puts it this way:

> Performance management is not just managing the performance of the individual, but managing the performance of the corporation as a whole, understanding what's working and what's not working, understanding what needs to be corrected, understanding how [teams, departments, functions, and business units] are performing, looking at the chain of accountabilities, and actively managing the chain of accountabilities. When the chain of accountabilities is not in place, people are sent in all sorts of directions to perform at counter-purposes to one another, and building a context of high-level competition that is disabling to many individuals.[1]

Because of its importance to the knowledge-enabled organization, the employee learning contract must be developed through a structured process that ensures the contract meets the needs of the company and the employee. Figure 4.1 specifies the five steps in developing an employee learning contract. In this chapter, we study each step and discuss how the learning contract differs from the more traditional employee development and training plans.

Figure 4.1. Five steps in developing an employee learning contract.

Step 1:
Determine company business goals.

Step 2:
Determine business unit / department / functional goals based on company goals.

Step 3:
Determine individual employee goals and associated knowledge and skill requirements.

Step 4:
Assess employees' current knowledge and skill levels and compare to needs.

Step 5:
Develop employee learning goals and contract.

Step 1: Determine Company Business Goals

For employee learning contracts to relate directly to the company's business goals, every employee must understand those goals. In too many companies, rank-and-file employees never see business goals, or if they do see the goals they are not understandable. Too often, top leaders consider the goals "too important" to share at the lowest levels of the company. In other companies, leaders keep the goals secret because they fear that competitors may obtain access to the information, or because they believe that holding the goals secret gives them power, or because they don't believe that sharing the goals at lower levels serves any purpose. Chapter 7 discusses in greater detail these effective barriers to establishment of a knowledge-enabled organization.

For the knowledge-enabled organization to succeed, the company's business goals must be:

* Written in clear, measurable language
* Widely communicated throughout the company
* Translatable into knowledge and skill requirements

Writing Goals in Clear, Measurable Language

Company goals are frequently written as lofty platitudes that can never be measured and are very difficult for most employees to understand. When was the last time you heard an employee present a new idea and comment, "This is sure to maximize our shareholders' return on equity!"? While the company's chief financial officer clearly understands what the term means, it is meaningless to many employees. And if employees cannot understand the company's goals, how can they work to achieve them? Gary Wuslich, president at AM General Corp. of South Bend, Indiana, remarks that expressions such as ". . . 'to become the dominant company in the markets we serve,' 'to be known for innovation, pioneering technology, and quality,' do not communicate the operational priorities and requirements that individuals can attack."[2]

Goals must be written in clear, measurable terms, using language that employees can understand and use to measure their own contributions to the company—for example: "We will introduce twenty new products in the next year"; "We will reduce the cost of manufacturing our products by 18 percent over the next two years"; "We will reduce the time to process a new account from three days to three hours during the next year." But even a company doing this may need to provide some basic business education so that employees can understand the business.

Few employees understand the general business language in which a company's goals are written. Rather, employees are generally well-versed only in the language of their own function, department, or business unit. How many employees understand the company's business statements, the income statement, or the balance sheet? How many understand the concepts of time-to-market, customer satisfaction, market segments, quality measures, and other terms commonly used in specifying business goals?

It behooves the company to educate all employees so that they can understand the basic business(es) in which the company is engaged, the major business processes on which the work is based, and the common terms used to describe the business and its goals. Without providing this basic education, companies cannot expect their employees to work toward achievement of those goals, or to make daily decisions supporting not only their own personal and departmental goals but also the company's overall goals.

This is what Jack Stack, president of Springfield Remanufacturing, in Springfield, Illinois, did when he invented The Great Game of Business.[3] Stack taught every company employee to read and understand the company's financial statements. He then organized employees into teams and gave them those statements on a regular basis with the goal of finding ways to improve business results. Without basic education on how to read financial statements, and without developing an understanding of how each employee's work affected the numbers in those statements, Stack's "great game of business" could never have succeeded.

Communicating Goals Throughout the Company

If your employees don't know what the company's goals are, how can they work toward their achievement? Few companies make the effort to communicate their goals widely throughout all levels of the organization. Some still believe that goal setting is an executive responsibility and that workers at lower levels should just do their jobs and leave the thinking to those at the higher levels.

In other companies, goal setting is seen as merely an annual planning exercise. Plans are made because "we do it every year" and "we need something to show to the board of directors." But then the plans are filed until next year's planning exercise. In these companies, there is little point in communicating goals to the rank and file because they have no meaning and cannot provide guidance to anyone. Today's successful companies ensure that stated goals are real and challenging but attainable, and that each employee in the company understands not only the stated goals but also his or her role in helping the company achieve those goals.

Writing in *Industry Week,* Mark A. Frohman advises:

> Ensure that people understand the purpose, plans, and priorities of the business and their part in carrying them out. This requires more than a newsletter from the president or a special meeting. It involves conveying the plans and priorities so that people can relate to the "big canvas" and see what they can do with their paint brushes. This means two-way communications; executives must answer questions about the strategy and priorities from people in the organization to ensure their grasp of it. Without this interaction, people cannot recognize unexpected problems or unexpected opportunities that they can act on.[4]

Translating Goals Into Knowledge and Skill Requirements

Every goal should be translatable into knowledge and skill requirements. Does the company want to improve time-to-market for new products? Then it has to learn to improve the product development process, so as to squeeze excess time and work from the process. Does the company want to enter a new market? Then it must learn about the new market, the needs and desires of customers in that market, the competitors it will face in that market, how to apply its core competencies to meet those needs, and so forth.

Step 2: Determine Business Unit/ Department/Functional Goals Based on Company Goals

Although employees must understand the company's business goals, their individual goals are based more on the goals of their individual departments, functions, or business units. This requires a cascade, where the company goals are translated for each of the company's departments, functions, and business units, all of which must support the overall goals of the company. (This is what CIBC's Saint-Onge calls the "chain of accountabilities.") In many companies, where the business goals are not taken seriously, goal setting at lower levels is done independently of company plans, and no one ever examines whether the sum of the parts equals the whole. This is a failure of both the planning process and company leadership.

Departmental, functional, and business unit goals must be derived directly from company goals. They must support the achievement of those larger goals, and they must be examined to ensure that the sum of the parts indeed enables the company to achieve its overall goals. Thus the major business processes must be fully understood, and each department, function, and business unit has to understand its role in those processes. Interdependencies among these groups must also be highlighted, and plans must be jointly made to ensure the achievement of goals that stretch beyond group boundaries.

Once goals are set at this level, they must be translated into knowledge and skill requirements. Start by determining what changes need to occur to reach the goal, and then look at the knowledge and skills required for such changes. For example, if the customer telephone response unit has a goal to improve customer satisfaction ratings by 10 percent, you must determine how this will happen: Do operators need better customer communication skills? Does the department need to develop better knowledge databases containing common questions and answers so that customers get the right answer more quickly? Or does the department need to work with the technical writing staff to correct errors or omissions in customer manuals? Once the group's knowledge and skill requirements are determined, then move on to the learning needs of the individual members of the group.

Step 3: Determine Individual Employee Goals and Associated Knowledge and Skill Requirements

The learning contract is an individual document for each employee. While there may be some commonalities for employees doing similar jobs, each individual is unique and must be treated uniquely. It is the manager's job to take the group's goals and the knowledge and skill requirements flowing from those goals and break them down into goals and requirements for each employee. In the example of the customer telephone support unit, all employees might need to learn how to use a new question-and-answer database. But one member of the group could be given responsibility for collecting information on documentation problems and communicating them to the technical writing department. Another employee or team of employees could be responsible for keeping the database up to date, or for starting a new database for a newly released product. Still others may have responsibility for surveying customers to get feedback on the service provided by the group.

The manager's job is to look at the changes needed to achieve the group's goals, assign responsibilities to group members, and work with each employee to assess the knowledge and skills needed to make the change happen. To do this most effectively, the manager should work through the process with employees, not determine and impose changes from above. It is the employees on the front line who best understand the work they do and the problems inherent in that work. Often, those front-line employees also know better than their managers what needs to change and how best to implement any change.

Step 4: Assess Employees' Current Knowledge and Skill Levels and Compare to Needs

Once the needed levels of knowledge and skills have been determined, you must then assess each employee's current levels. Otherwise, you end up wasting time and resources providing pointless learning activities.

> A graduate student in one of my classes recently took a job as director of technical support at a fast-growth high-tech manufacturer. On his first day on the job, he was told that he had to sign up for a three-day time management program, a required course for all new employees. "If they want me to manage my time effectively, and that's never been a problem for me," he told me, "my first decision would be not to attend that course. There are probably 10–20 percent of employees in any company who really need to take a time management course. For the rest, it is a waste of time and money."

You also have to avoid the trap of assuming that employees have skills and knowledge that they don't. If employees appear to be getting the job done, we assume that they are doing it in the most efficient and effective manner. For example, one company had for years color-coded the packaging of parts. Then, in trying to reduce expenses, someone decided to use uniform, single-color packaging for all parts. Suddenly, those employees who had relied on the color coding instead of learning the part numbers were lost, and they started shipping incorrect orders. The resulting costs were much greater than the savings gained by standardizing the color scheme.

> While doing a sales training needs assessment at a financial services company, I asked the sales vice-president how her salespeople got competitive information. "For example," I remarked, "I've seen several very

complimentary articles about your company in the trade press in the past month. Do you have a mechanism to collect and disseminate this type of information to your people?"

"Oh, they get all the information they need," she replied. "They all keep up with the trade press on their own."

When I asked her how the sales force shared experiences with each other, I got a similar response: "They just pick up the phone and call each other when they need to."

When I surveyed the sales force, I found that neither of these assumptions was true. Sales reps were too busy trying to make their quotas and win sales awards to spend time keeping up with their own company or their major competitors, much less the trade press, and the only time they talked with each other was at the semiannual sales meetings.

Errors on either side can be costly. We might assume that employees have knowledge and skills that in fact they don't have. Or that they don't have knowledge and skills that in fact they do have. The only way to make certain that the learning contract for each employee is correct is to do an honest assessment of what the employee does and does not know.

Step 5: Develop Employee Learning Goals and Contract

Once the manager has analyzed the gaps in knowledge and skills that must be filled in order to meet the group's business goals, she must then work with individual employees to determine individual goals and learning contracts. There are two important points to remember in doing this:

1. There may be alternatives to individual learning goals that should be considered. In addition to developing new knowledge and skills within the group, the manager also has

the option of buying those skills (for example, by hiring a new employee who already has the needed knowledge and skills), or renting them (by hiring a consultant or a contract employee for a specified period of time). To make these decisions, managers should use criteria such as how quickly the knowledge and skills are needed, what levels of knowledge and skills are needed, and how long will they be needed.[5]

2. The manager must make certain that the sum of the knowledge and skills of her employees, both current levels and those to be developed, is sufficient to attain the group's business goals. It is all too easy to develop a reasonable learning contract for each employee, only to discover later that some specific knowledge or skill lacking in the group as a whole prevents achieving a goal.

Developing an Employee Learning Contract: Employee and Manager Roles

The learning contract is jointly developed by each employee and his or her manager. The first responsibility belongs to the manager, namely to describe for each employee a set of job requirements, including changes required to meet next year's goals. To accomplish this, the manager works from the group's goals (based on company goals) to determine roles and goals for each employee. Next, the manager lists the competencies needed by each employee to fulfill those roles and meet those goals. Once this is done, the manager communicates this information to each employee.

The employee's responsibility is to learn from the manager about the group's goals and the role that the manager has in mind for the employee in helping to meet those goals. The employee should then develop her own list of the competencies she feels are needed to fulfill that role. When she completes her competency list, she should then meet with the manager to compare their respective lists and reach agreement on individual goals, roles, and competencies.

Once the destination is agreed upon, the employee and her

manager then agree on the employee's current level of competencies. Both the manager and the employee should, separately, complete an assessment form, judging the employee's current levels on each of the competencies needed to do the job. After completing the task separately, they meet to compare, discuss, and negotiate to reach agreement. Then, by comparing current and needed levels, they identify the gaps needing to be filled, identify what types of learning activities the employee might undertake to fill those gaps, and assign priorities to the learning requirements.

The employee now takes the lead in developing the actual learning contract by identifying learning resources, planning learning activities, and developing a schedule for learning. This is also an area where the training or human resources development group can provide assistance to employees. CIBC has developed an excellent Individual Development Planner to help its employees with this process (see Figure 4.2).

Competency Models to Support the Learning Contract

It is much easier for the manager and employee to make a learning contract if the company develops competency models for specific jobs. CIBC, Caterpillar, PPG Industries, and many other large companies have spent many years and large amounts of money developing models that specify the competencies for major job classifications. CIBC, for example, has developed a comprehensive set of competency models for employees in the branch network of their personal and commercial banking operations. For each job in a particular job group, the model specifies required knowledge and skills, grouped into three broad categories:

1. *Relational competencies.* These competencies are the knowledge and skills that help you work with and through others. Examples: interpersonal relations; people management and development.
2. *Business competencies.* These competencies are the knowledge and skills that help drive commercial success (i.e.,

Figure 4.2. Questions from CIBC's individual development planner.

✳ What do I want to learn?

- Record the competency titles you have identified as priorities, and the knowledge and skill statements you have labeled "immediate."

  Example:
  Group Dynamics
  —Knowledge of the principles and various techniques of teamwork.
  —Be supportive of the team and team members.

✳ How am I going to learn it?

- Plan the activities that can help you develop the knowledge and skills you want to learn.
- Consider how you like to learn; how you learn best; who may help you—choose from assignments, readings, courses, etc.
- Identify when you plan to do these activities.

  Example:
  —Obtain literature on teamwork (e.g., *Team Players and Teamwork*, G. M. Parker). (January)
  —Discuss with team leader and members what I can do to be more supportive of the team. (February)

✳ How will I know I learned it?

- Ask yourself "How do I know I don't need to do any more development—I've learned it?"
- Think about what will show you that you successfully learned what you planned to learn.

  Example:
  —I will outline the principles and techniques of teamwork to my manager.
  —Feedback in six months from team leader/members indicates I am supportive of the team without need for reminders and coaching.

"run the business—any business"). Examples: business planning; problem solving and decision making.

3. *Technical competencies.* These competencies are specific to a particular job group (e.g., branch network, financial accounting) and help drive excellence within that function. Examples: product knowledge; providing financial solutions.[6]

When competency models exist, they simplify the work of managers and employees, allowing them to prepare their competency lists from the profiles and to measure achievement of competencies against the criteria listed in the profiles. Because goals, jobs, and conditions constantly change, the competency profiles are meant to be used as a good, general guide and can be modified by either employee or manager depending on the needs of the individual and the group. An example of a competency profile used by CIBC is shown in Figure 4.3.

Integrating Learning Into the Job

In the learning model presented in Chapter 2, I said that information can be transformed into knowledge only by applying it to the job. Integrating the employee's learning into changes in how he does his work is the key to individual and company success and is the primary way in which the learning contract differs from traditional employee development plans.

The employee has primary responsibility for this integration, but the manager must play an active role in ensuring that newly learned information and skills are correctly applied and that their application to the employee's work actually is helping to meet the group's goals. The manager must act as a coach, watching the employee's work performance and providing advice, tips, and feedback on how well he is doing. Says Barrie Whittaker, general manager of AMP of Canada Ltd.: "The manager must allow employees a time and place for practicing their skills. Practice allows employees to build on their capabilities and understanding in a systematic way. Errors are welcomed with understanding and compassion, and employees are redirected toward improved performance."[7]

Figure 4.3. Sample competency profile.

Problem Solving and Decision Making

> The knowledge of problem-solving and decision-making techniques, and the ability to generate solutions to problems, and decide on a course of action.

Know and understand:

❏ 1. Processes for systematically identifying, analyzing, and generating alternatives to issues/problems (e.g., group problem solving.

❏ 2. Processes for making decisions.

❏ 3. When and who should make the decision and when to refer, delegate, or elevate it.

Be able to:

❏ 4. Spot patterns or trends that indicate potential problems/issues.

❏ 5. Identify an existing problem/issue, take ownership for follow-through.

❏ 6. Relate problem/issue to other experiences to identify common themes.

❏ 7. Determine the root cause of the problem.

❏ 8. Evaluate potential impact/risks of problems.

❏ 9. Generate alternatives to resolve problems (even where there is no policy or precedent), and determine pros and cons of alternatives.

❏ 10. Balance short-term needs and/or pressures for quick solutions with long-term needs and/or requirements for quality.

❏ 11. Evaluate solutions in terms of their business, financial, and customer-service impacts, and CIBC values.

❏ 12. Choose the best alternative.

❏ 13. Encourage innovative and calculated risk taking while striving for an error-free environment.

❏ 14. Identify potential barriers; remove or work around them to implement solutions.

❏ 15. Recognize when you have the authority to make decisions, and either make them (even when it will not be a popular one) or refer them to the appropriate level.

The manager also continuously monitors the overall work of the group and its progress toward the group's goals. Even if a newly learned work method is designed to solve a particular problem or improve work efficiency, the actual results from applying that method may not meet expectations. Other factors can inhibit the individual employee and the group as a whole from meeting their goals. It is the manager's role to monitor progress and work with the group to identify why things might not be working as expected, and to develop alternative plans as needed.

Features of the Learning Contract

A sample form for a learning contract is shown in Figure 4.4.

Each employee's learning contract is unique. It may be more than one page, depending on the number of business goals being addressed.

The learning contract differs from the traditional employee development plan in several important ways, besides those already addressed. It has sections on:

* Measures of learning achievement
* How learning will be applied to the job
* Business results expected

Each of these sections is vital to the knowledge-enabled organization.

Measures of Learning Achievement

In traditional organizations, when an employee is sent to a training program it is assumed that she learned whatever the training program offered. Few training organizations test employees on how much they actually learned, unless there are specific requirements for such testing, for example, in training nuclear power plant operators, or if the training supports a competency system (and even then, many companies assume that comple-

Figure 4.4. Learning contract form.

Employee_____ Manager _____

Period covered: _____ , 19 ____ to _____ , 19____

Business Goal #_____:

Employee's role and responsibilities in meeting business goal:

Competencies needed for specified role and responsibilities:

Gaps between current and desired competencies:

Learning Plan to Fill Gaps
   Learning method(s):

   Schedule for learning activities:

   Measure of learning achievement:

   How learning will be applied to the job:

   Business results expected:

tion of training is sufficient to check off the competency in the employee's record).

The knowledge-enabled organization recognizes that whatever the employee learns, whether through a formal training program or by other means, does not become the employee's knowledge until she applies it to her job. The measure of learning achieved is, therefore, the demonstration of new knowledge or skills that can be applied to the job.

Look back at Figure 4.3, the sample competency profile from CIBC. The measures of learning for problem solving and decision making are specific understanding and capabilities. Such a competency profile is a starting point for this section, but the learning contract must tie learning to specific business goals. To go back to the example of the customer telephone support unit, the "measure of learning achieved" might specify that the employee develop a problem resolution procedure for customer complaints, or a procedure for referring to the documentation group any question that arises more than ten times in the first three months of supporting a new product.

Applying Learning to the Job

In most companies, the employee development plan never addresses how learning is applied to the employee's job, so most training attended by employees never gets applied. In the learning contract, the employee and her manager must specify how newly acquired skills and knowledge will be applied to the job. This requires more of a change for the manager than for the employee.

Employees who find their learning experience of value are anxious to apply their new knowledge and skills. But because this application takes time and almost certainly requires practice and inevitable errors, the employee needs a supportive manager who tolerates some amount of error, allows extra time, and provides the coaching and reinforcement needed to ensure that the learning is correctly applied. As stated by Whittaker of Canada's AMP:

> Managers must constantly coach and assess their employees until they demonstrate the ability to carry out

the task themselves to an acceptable standard of performance. Detecting the point at which this occurs is not an easy task. People learn at different rates, and thus must be considered individually in assessing their readiness for a task. When employees have retained a reliable set of practices, show sincere commitment to the new practice, and demonstrate the necessary level of competence, then the coach can trust and empower them.[8]

This section of the learning contract thus ensures that the employee and the manager agree on how the employee's learning is applied to the job.

Business Results Expected

Because the learning contract is directly tied to business goals, any learning activity undertaken should lead to a positive change in business results. The learning contract specifies those expectations. I have yet to see a traditional employee development plan that specifies expected business results; but if you can't specify the expected results, you can't assign responsibility for them.

Notes

1. Saint-Onge is quoted from a personal interview.
2. Mark A. Frohman, "Unleash Urgency and Action," *Industry Week* (CompuServe online edition), November 4, 1996.
3. Jack Stack, *The Great Game of Business* (New York: Currency Doubleday, 1992).
4. Frohman, op. cit.
5. For a more complete discussion of the buy-versus-rent-versus-development criteria, see Daniel R. Tobin, *Transformational Learning: Renewing Your Company Through Knowledge and Skills* (New York: John Wiley & Sons, 1996, especially Chapter 7).
6. From *The Individual Development Process Workbook—Branch Network* (Toronto: Canadian Imperial Bank of Commerce, 1993, p. 21). Used by permission.

7. Barrie Whittaker, "Shaping the Competitive Organization—Managing or Coaching?" *CMA Magazine*, April 1993, p. 5. Used with permission of The Society of Management Accountants of Canada.
8. Ibid.

5

Learning to Get the Job Done

The man who has ceased to learn ought not to be allowed to wander around loose in these dangerous days.

M. M. Coady

Learning activities can take many forms, including but not limited to traditional approaches to training.

Let's start with a brief definition of learning in the context of the knowledge-enabled organization. Learning is the acquisition of the knowledge and skills necessary to meet individual, group, and company goals. Here is a more operational definition of learning, using the learning model from Chapter 2: *Learning is the act of finding relevant information and applying it to the employee's work to make a positive difference in business results.*

From this definition, it follows that learning must be employee-driven, rather than company-imposed. It is the employee who best understands the content and context of her work and, therefore, can make the best judgment as to what information is relevant. It is also the employee who must apply that information to her work and who is measured on her ability to get the job done based on what she has learned. So, rather than limit employees to a structured catalog of training programs defined and developed by a corporate training group, it is important to open a wide array of learning opportunities (including traditional training programs) to each employee and let her decide what to learn and how best to learn.

This employee-centered approach to learning accommodates many learning styles and learning methods. Without trying to provide a complete taxonomy of styles and methods, let's look at how employees in a wide variety of jobs and companies are taking responsibility for their own learning. People learn in two basic ways: from other people, and by discovery.

How People Learn From Others

Our first learning comes from our parents and caregivers. We learn language, customs, and basic skills as we develop from infancy through childhood into adulthood. We are taught by example, through language and symbol, but all this learning depends on having a teacher, be that parent, sibling, friend, or schoolteacher. We learn from writers whose books we read, artists whose work we see, craftsmen whose work we touch, and cooks whose work we taste and smell. Sometimes, we are taught directly (listen to me and learn what I say); more often we learn remotely, from what the teacher has created or left for us to learn from. As a young child, our learning is directed by parents and teachers. As we grow, we become more self-directed in our learning activities.

When we become employees of a corporation, we continue to learn in these same ways:

* By attending classes where we are taught directly
* Through on-the-job training, where we are shown what to do and how to do it
* By watching a videotape, listening to an audiotape, or using a computer-based or multimedia presentation that contains information we need
* By reading manuals and reports that have been written by people sharing their knowledge and experience

All of the above methods are company-directed. That is, in each example someone in the company has determined that there is a set of information that the employee must master and has deliberately created a formal delivery mechanism to impart the information. Such mechanisms can be effective, but they can only cover explicit knowledge, information that is easily represented in written or verbal form.

Even more than through these formal mechanisms, employees obtain the information they need through informal learning methods:

* By asking a question of a manager or colleague who has more knowledge and experience
* By observing how others (colleagues, managers, consultants, team members, etc.) do their work
* By discussing their own work with others who do similar or related work

These informal learning methods are not only desirable but absolutely essential to conveying tacit knowledge, knowledge that isn't easily represented in written form but that exists primarily in the minds of knowledgeable people.

Informal learning methods are essential to conveying tacit knowledge—knowledge that exists primarily in the minds of knowledgeable people.

To better understand the differences between these formal and informal methods of learning, let's examine how General Electric's Crotonville, New York, learning center helps promote the sharing (learning) of best practices among companies.

Learning About Best Practices Within GE: A Team Approach

Steve Kerr, GE's chief learning officer, tells how a best practice from GE's appliance group in Louisville, Kentucky, is shared with other GE operations.

If the Louisville best practice were totally straightforward and easy to implement, GE could ask a knowledgeable person in Louisville to write a training manual detailing the steps to implement the program. But, as with most corporate programs, there are many people involved, many cross-functional dependencies, a lot of synergy among people and groups who develop and implement the technique. Since much of the knowledge that these people develop is tacit in nature, they may not even recognize what they know and, therefore, could never actually write it down.

As Kerr tells the story:

> What do we do? We bring a team, maybe seven people, from Louisville to Crotonville: a finance person, a marketing person, a union shop steward, a sourcing person, an HR rep, etc. Then we bring in maybe eighty people from six different businesses to learn from the Louisville team. First, the team does a 10–15 minute quick overview of its business—it's a teaser. They don't give away much because we want the people to learn how to learn, not just learn. Then the seven appliance people go into separate rooms, where they answer questions from the eighty people, who have divided up into smaller groups.[1]

Kerr's strategy is not to force-feed information to the learners, but to stimulate them to learn by asking questions. The quick overview sets the context for the questions. Because the seven Louisville representatives all have different perspectives on the appliance program, based on their functional roles in that operation and their specific roles in the development and implementation of the program, each of them has knowledge that the other six people don't. If the session were held as a large panel discussion and someone from another GE group asked a question, one appliance person might answer the question. Another Louisville person might add something to the answer, but it is unlikely that all seven people would take the time to give their personal perspectives in answer to each question. By having each representative work with a different group in a different room, there is time to hear the perspective of each—to bring out each person's tacit knowledge.

At the same time, by design the executives from other plants are unable to attend the sessions of all seven Louisville people. The team from any of the GE facilities represented in the audience has to decide which person attends which session (actually, each person gets to attend two sessions) to gather information. Then each learning team meets to share what they learn and to discuss how they might apply their learning to their own operation. After each learning team has come up with its own plan, Kerr says,

> [W]e bring them back into a big room and they present what they think were the keys to Louisville's success. Then we turn to the Louisville group and ask: "What questions didn't they ask? What part of your transformation is a success that they did not figure out?" And they offer all sorts of useful suggestions: "Well, you know, they never asked us how we did training. They never asked about the relationships with suppliers, and that was the key." And so on.[2]

The sagacity of Kerr's approach to learning includes five important points that are missing from most of today's corporate training programs:

1. *The program of sharing best practices is a strategic business initiative.* By bringing together teams from a variety of GE business units, the company ensures that each of these business units recognizes they must implement this program for alignment with corporate goals. The design of the program tells participants what they are expected to accomplish, but not how to do it. Essentially, GE says: "We want you to implement this program that was started in Louisville. Come learn from the Louisville people, but then develop your own plans to accomplish this as you see best."

2. *The program focuses on the learners' needs and the actual business problems they face in their own operations.* No one claims to be able to identify the learning needs of participants from many different functional roles in their respective business units and package the needed learning in a "one size fits all" learning

solution. Instead, participants direct their own learning, based on their roles and responsibilities in their own business units.

3. *The program is interactive, with participants drawing out the information they need to do their own jobs.* Rather than being lecture-based or trainer-directed, the program allows for questions and responses. Where the responses don't answer the question, there is follow-up. And at the end, the knowledge resources (the people from Louisville) themselves are asked to judge whether any relevant questions have not been asked and to fill in those gaps for the participants.

4. *The program allows participants to determine the value of the information received in the context of their own businesses.* The appliance people do not stand up and say: "This is the right way to do things. You have to do it the way we did." Rather, they offer their own experiences and let the participants determine what would be of value to them.

5. *Since a team-based approach is needed, the program sends a team to learn about it.* The company ensures that a team of people, rather than one individual, drives implementation in each target business unit. Each team member brings his or her own perspective to the program, and each learns different information. The goal is to provide synergy at the business unit level as team members bring their different perspectives and talents to the planning for the local implementation effort. Team members also provide reinforcement for each other throughout the planning and implementation process.

In short, this is a well-designed, learner-centered approach to knowledge transfer that allows participants to gain not just the explicit knowledge that could be placed in a training manual or formal training program, but also the tacit knowledge of the people actually involved in the development and implementation of the transformation program. Because the learner-participants meet the Louisville people, they can later follow up with them by telephone or e-mail as they think of other questions or face problems in their own implementation efforts. And because each targeted business unit is represented by a team, the connections made are more numerous and stronger, not just business unit to business unit, but function to function, team member to team member.

Learning Management Skills at Brigham and Women's Hospital

At Boston's Brigham and Women's Hospital, the top management team was concerned with the basic management competencies within the hospital's management staff. The hospital's Healthcare Learning Group took a unique approach to encourage learning among the management staff, working with top hospital management to identify a set of core competencies for all hospital managers. Then, working with the senior management team and her own knowledge of the hospital administrative staff, group manager Terry Wagner formed teams of top performers in each of these competency areas.

After receiving training, each team was charged with creating learning tools to help promote the development of these competencies across all administrative groups. At the same time, the team members became knowledge resources for other administrators in the hospital.

The teams used a wide variety of approaches to disseminate their knowledge:

* The performance management/coaching team developed a competency rating form for BWH exempt-employee performance appraisal.
* The change management team developed the "BWH Compass," a management tool for implementing change.
* The analytical/systems-thinking team developed a decision-making model.
* The customer-orientation team introduced customer service standards using a pamphlet and a video.

These unique approaches to sharing knowledge, mostly neither system-based nor in the form of traditional training programs, illustrate building a knowledge network: sharing the knowledge of an organization's top performers to help others learn and to improve the overall performance of the organization.

While Brigham and Women's Hospital utilized a variety of methods to share the knowledge of top performers, the choice of methods was left up to the producers of the materials. In the ideal world, the choice of methods is determined by the needs of the learners, rather than the preferences of the teachers.

Learning the Job at ABB Industrial Systems: An Individual Approach

At ABB Industrial Systems in Columbus, Ohio, shop employees have learned to take charge of the manufacturing process. To accomplish this replacement of supervised functional teams with high-performance work teams, employees needed to learn about the manufacturing process and to acquire the skills to analyze and control that process. According to George Morris, vice-president of manufacturing and supply management, this started with "one up/one down" skill training: "One of our goals is for all employees to learn the skills of the person who gives them the work-in-process product, and those of their immediate customer."[3]

In many companies, cross-training of production employees is done to provide flexibility. If workers know how to do more than one job, they can fill in when others are absent or when there is a bottleneck in one part of the manufacturing process. At ABB, there is an additional goal: each employee understands at least a three-step piece of the overall manufacturing process. The approach is working for ABB. Says laser-alignment technician Dan Dudley, "Being in control is a powerful tool for those closest to the process. It enables us to act and prevent problems that we see coming."[4]

Learning About Customers at EMC

EMC Corp. has a real focus on understanding their customers. In most companies, customer contact is limited to salespeople, field personnel, and occasional executive visits. But EMC wants all employees to learn about customers and provides many ways to do it: "[S]hare customer letters and surveys with everyone, send people to customer sites, have as many people as possible meet customers when they visit, use the sales force to introduce customers and explain competition, and invite a few customers in to address employees."[5]

These practices at EMC make it possible for employees to learn. The company's job is to make these learning resources available to employees. The employees' responsibility is to match the available learning resources to their learning requirements and select those that best enable them to do their jobs.

Using Knowledge Networks to Enable Learning From Others

Many companies today are building knowledge repositories and networks to enable employees to learn from others. A knowledge repository or database collects and provides access to information about employees' experiences. For example, the *California Management Review* reports that architectural engineering giant Bechtel "has defined and implemented structured knowledge processes to ensure that its project teams bring to their design decision making all the benefits of discoveries made by other project teams past and present."[6] Such a knowledge database can, of course, only contain explicit knowledge.

K'Netix®, The Buckman Knowledge Network™, contains not only an extensive library of case studies of unusual applications of products from Buckman Laboratories (representing explicit knowledge) but also a set of interactive forums through which Buckman employees can ask questions, start discussions, and get answers from others. The dynamic nature of these discussion forums is important because continued questioning and discussion uncover tacit knowledge.

We discuss knowledge networks, including Buckman's K'Netix®, at greater length in Chapter 6.

Learning by Discovery

When a child wants to learn to ride a bicycle, she doesn't do it by reading a book or listening to someone tell her how. She gets on the bike and discovers how to do it. Yes, she may receive coaching from a parent before and during her first attempts, and, yes, her parents may put training wheels on the bicycle to keep the learning environment safe for her. But she can learn to ride only by trying it, by discovering how to maintain balance while pedaling, how to shift weight during turns, how to apply both brake levers at the same time. Learning by discovery also means that she makes errors and she falls. The parent's role is to help her learn from mistakes and to encourage her to keep practicing until she is comfortable and has mastered the necessary skills. Can the child learn by herself, without teaching and coaching? Probably. But that takes a child who is either impervious to pain or who has learned to reflect on and learn from her own mistakes.

Just as we cannot expect anyone to instantaneously master bicycle riding, we also cannot expect employees to acquire new information, learn new skills, and then immediately apply them perfectly to the job. We must allow the employee to test out the new ideas and skills. We provide a learning environment that helps the employee learn from mistakes and provides coaching and reinforcement until he is ready to fly solo; parents don't punish the child for falling off the bike. Even after attending a traditional training program or using a computer-based or multimedia learning program, employees still have to discover how the content relates to their work; they must practice applying newly acquired information and skills before they can productively and reliably use them. It is common to observe the "Aha!" phenomenon whereby an employee starts applying their learning to the job and suddenly "discovers" what the course content really means and how it really works.

For example, when a work team starts to analyze the processes it controls and plans for changes to those processes, they cannot know exactly how their ideas will work until they apply them, discover what works and what doesn't, and then fine-tune those processes. Experimentation and discovery don't take place just in the research laboratory; they occur every time an employee tries out a new idea, applies new information to his work, or tries out a newly learned skill.

Managers must allow for experimentation, time to test and

master new skills. They should trust that employees are capable of mastering new skills and adding value to the business. Managers also have to recognize that when they empower employees to use their own knowledge and skills, rather than directing employees to just follow orders from others, they can unleash tremendous power that can propel people to new levels of achievement. Mark Koskiniemi, vice-president of human resources at Buckman Laboratories, says, "When a supervisor approves or suggests a learning activity, he needs to understand that he too is making a commitment to supporting that learning activity."

At Chesebrough-Pond's Jefferson City, Missouri, plant, the design of a new production line was done locally with the full participation of the production employees who would eventually run the operation. In many companies, production employees would never be let near such plans if management felt that only higher-level industrial engineers and managers could engage in such important work. In this case, the production employees "were involved in layout, actual installation, and testing," and according to industrial engineer Leo McCarthy,

> a significant objective was to ensure that a size change-over could occur within thirty minutes. Using this as an objective, the line personnel examined every opportunity for improvement and were empowered to make changes as appropriate. The result: Line changeovers occur in less than fifteen minutes, making changeovers a nonissue.[7]

By examining "every opportunity for improvement," these Chesebrough-Pond employees have learned by discovery.

How to Learn to Get the Job Done

Any employee seeking to fulfill the requirements of the learning contract must go through four steps:

1. Find the right learning resource to match the learning requirement.

2. Learn.
3. Apply the learning to the job.
4. Measure the results.

Finding the Right Learning Resources

Learning resources can take many forms. A learning resource is any source of relevant data (information): a person, a book, case studies in a database, a course, etc. Traditional forms include:

* A company training course
* A course at a local college or university, or a workshop sponsored by a professional organization
* A book on the subject
* A video or audio program on the subject
* A computer-based or multimedia instructional program

Each of these learning resources requires someone other than the learner to have anticipated the learning need and invested in developing the needed instruction. Thus the employee who relies totally on these learning methods is at the mercy of those who created the programs. The creator(s) of programs might have no idea what challenges the employee is facing, might never have actually done work like that being required of the employee, and generally might have no concept of what any one employee's preferred method of learning or schedule for learning is. So when employees rely on these external learning resources, they are forced to conform to preprogrammed expectations on learning styles, methods of instruction, required course content, and schedule.

Less formal, more nontraditional forms of learning include:

* Asking someone who has the skill or knowledge to teach it to you. This can be done informally, if the time required for learning is minimal, or in the more formal manner of job rotation or apprenticeship if learning time is more extensive.

* Doing personal research on the subject. An employee interested in a new manufacturing technique can do a library or Internet search for articles, papers, or books on the new tech-

nique. He may find another business, or another division of his own company, that is using the technique and ask to visit its operation. He may ask a university researcher who has developed the technique to come to the company to demonstrate and discuss it.

* Finding other people with the same learning need and planning how they can all learn together. If an employee discovers that others share her learning need, she can organize a learning group to use any of these nontraditional methods to create learning materials—as well as contracting with an internal or external training group to create a formal training program for the group.

Employees are responsible for finding their own learning resources, but their managers and their companies can greatly facilitate this process. Managers can use their wider base of experience and networks of people in the company to help employees identify and access learning resources, whether courses, project reports, or people. The company can provide learning counselors or learning centers where employees can go to research and find a variety of learning resources.

Joseph Slezak, manager of training and development at Mercury Marine in Fond du Lac, Wisconsin, has built an exemplary employee learning center that contains a wide variety of audio- and videotapes, computer-based and multimedia training programs, books, and other learning materials. Slezak also utilizes learning counselors from the University of Wisconsin to provide free, confidential counseling to employees seeking ways to acquire new knowledge and skills. At the Canadian Imperial Bank of Commerce, Hubert Saint-Onge has created a series of career centers across the company. Within these career centers are learning counselors whose job it is to help employees find the learning resources they need.

Learning

Once the best learning resources are found, it is up to the employee to undertake the learning activity. Whether by listening, watching, discussing, or doing, it is the employee's responsibility to gather the information or learn the skill that he needs to fulfill the learning contract.

A very effective approach is called "action learning," in which employees apply the content as they are learning it. Rather than using hypothetical case studies, employees tackle real, work-related problems, applying the new knowledge and skills to solving the problem as they learn. (This approach actually combines this step with the next one: applying learning to the job.)

Many companies have combined team training with a type of "war room" exercise in which a group of employees simultaneously learns team skills and solves a pressing business problem. In this type of learning program, the group works as a team on a pressing business issue, for example, designing a new product, introducing a new service, or reengineering a business process. One or more trainer-consultants work with the team to provide just-in-time learning around team skills. Other consultants may be brought it as necessary to instruct the team on planning methodologies, process mapping, or other skills the team needs. Over a period of a week to several months, the team lives together and works exclusively on the problem. One of the trainer-consultants constantly monitors the team's work, acting sometimes as a facilitator, sometimes as a coach, and sometimes as an instructor, always making certain that the team's learning needs are met. The team works over this period in their war room or "situation room"—reminiscent of Pentagon or other federal government crisis control centers.

This type of action learning program can be very effective, but it also has some associated risks, primarily that when the program has been designed and implemented, the team may be disbanded, leaving no one in the company with the knowledge of how to continue the effort or to solve future problems related to the program.

A computer company put together a "situation team," composed primarily of headquarters-based engineers, marketers, and planners, to bid on a special project to design a computer network for the retail branches of a large metropolitan bank. The team did an outstanding job on the proposal and won the business. A second team was assembled to build and install the network (including several custom-designed components) and get it up and running. On completion of their work, each team was disbanded and its members went back to their respective jobs.

Several months later, a problem arose with the network. The bank called its local contact for field service. The field service technicians looked at the nonstandard installation and said they had no idea how to even determine what the problem was. The special teams had done an outstanding job in winning the business and in doing the original installation, but they had left behind no knowledge for others who would need to service the network and keep it running over time.

Applying Learning to the Job

This is the key step in transforming learning into knowledge. It is also the step in which companies tend to lose the benefits of their investment in training and other learning activities. Too often, companies fail to let employees apply their new knowledge and skills to the job. Or when the inevitable problems arise as the new learning changes work methods, they abandon the new approaches in favor of the old, which "may not be the most modern ways of getting things done, but they've worked for years."

The question still remains as to how to overcome this situation. There are several ways of avoiding this problem:

* Provide employees with a learning environment that doesn't punish failure but instead encourages them to continue learning until the new knowledge and skills have been mastered.
* When a group is trying to learn new skills or work methods, have more than one employee engage in the learning activity. In this way, they can reinforce and coach each other.
* Ensure that learning resources remain available to pro-

vide answers and coaching to employees who are trying to introduce new ways of doing business. One key in providing this type of ongoing support is to build a knowledge network (see Chapter 6).

Measuring Results

Recall that the purpose of all learning activities is to enable the company and its employees to meet their collective and individual goals. Once the learning phase is completed and the employee has applied the learning to the job, it is time to determine whether the learning has helped him meet his goals. Such measurement flows directly from the learning contract described in Chapter 4. Following the procedures for developing the learning contract usually yields positive results. But what if they are negative? What if there is no increase in productivity or quality, no decrease in time-to-market, no improvement in other specified measures?

With a negative result, you need to look at the cause of the deficiency. The easiest way to assign responsibility for the failure is to blame the employee, saying if she were a better learner, she would have better results. But things are not always as they first appear. The process can break down at any point along the way.

* You might not find the right learning resource. Unfortunately, along with excellent internal and external trainers, there are also many who are not good at their jobs. They may have inadequate training themselves, or they may be charlatans who claim to have knowledge or skills they don't have. You might identify a learning resource that is targeted at a different type of industry or work, and the translation into the employee's work may be poor. Finding the right learning resource for any learning need is not a trivial exercise. Without paying proper attention to the learning needs of the company and its employees, you can doom the learning process from the start.

* The employee might have difficulty learning. There may be a mismatch of teaching and learning styles between the learning resource and the learner. Perhaps the employee hasn't been

allowed enough time to master the material; I have seen employees attending an intensive training program while, at the same time, their managers have required them to continue doing their jobs as usual. Or, the employee or her manager might underestimate the amount of time needed to master the subject matter.

✳ The employee might not have sufficient time, or not have the needed coaching and reinforcement, to master application of the new material to the job. If the employee's manager or co-workers have a stake in the old work methods, the employee probably cannot succeed in introducing new methods.

✳ Incorrect measurements might be applied. It could be assumed that introduction of a new work method will yield a 20 percent increase in productivity while, realistically, a 10 percent improvement is all that can be expected. An incorrect original diagnosis of the problem can doom the learning prescription from the start. For example, employees may be taught statistical process control (SPC) to allow them to better control variances from specifications in the manufacturing process. But if the variance problem arises from outdated, worn-out equipment incapable of producing materials to specification, no amount of SPC training will solve the problem.

Applying the Model

In a discussion with a student in one of my graduate management classes, we developed the following scenario as a good illustration of this four-step process.

Deb is part of a systems group for a large, multifacility health center. She is responsible for implementing a new patient information system and for a network of trainers who provide individual training sessions for physicians on how to use the new system.

A new trainer, Max, was hired at a remote facility two months ago. Max started by identifying his own learning resources for the new job (Step 1). These included the systems manuals and documentation, and people who were knowledgeable about the system and the task of training physicians—that is, Deb and his local manager.

During his first two months, Max spent time learning (Step 2): reading the manuals, practicing using the system himself, attending a train-the-trainer session that Deb instructed, and shadowing Deb during several physician training sessions. Before doing his first solo session with a physician, he made a list of his own questions and reviewed them with his manager. He also used the hospital's teleconferencing system to do a practice session with Deb a hundred miles away. This type of practice gave Max an extra measure of confidence in preparing for his new role as trainer.

When he felt he was ready, Max made his first appointment with a local physician. Max did the presentation and his manager did the observing (Step 3, applying the learning to the job). When the session was over, Max's manager spent an hour with him reviewing the session and coaching him on the finer points. Since Max did an excellent job, his manager certified him to continue doing these training sessions without his presence. He emphasized that he would always be available to help answer questions that might arise.

The results of Max's learning were measured (Step 4) by the evaluation questionnaire completed by each physician at the end of the training session. Further evaluation came from monitoring how quickly the physician started using the patient information system after completion of the training.

Leveraging the Company's Knowledge Resources

The power of the knowledge-enabled organization comes from its ability to identify and harness all available knowledge resources and apply them to specific learning needs.

The key to employee and organizational learning lies in finding the right knowledge resources from which to learn. The knowledge resources within any company tend to be more numerous than anyone imagines. The power of the knowledge-enabled organization comes from its ability to identify and harness all of these knowledge resources and apply them to specific learning needs. Writing in *The Wall Street Journal*, David Bank says that employees hold a wealth of knowledge and experience about their company, from its products, customers, and competitors to its production processes and internal technology. But much of that knowledge is held in bits and pieces by various individuals or sections of the company. Banks writes:

> If these bits and pieces could be gathered and distributed throughout the entire company, the reasoning goes, the shared knowledge—a sort of collective IQ—would become a powerful force. Workers could use the pool of information to create competitive advantages and increase revenue. A company, for example, might discover that a process used in one sector could have applications in another. Or a company representative, using all of the company's knowledge about a customer, could make a superior presentation to the client, helping to seal a deal.[8]

Chapter 6 shows how building a knowledge network can support individual and organizational learning and can be a key ingredient in the development of the knowledge-enabled organization.

Notes

1. Richard M. Hodgetts, "A Conversation with Steve Kerr," *Organizational Dynamics*, Spring 1996, pp. 68–79.
2. Ibid.
3. Theodore Kinni, "America's Best Plants," *Industry Week* (CompuServe online edition), October 7, 1996.
4. Ibid.
5. Mark A. Frohman, "Unleash Urgency and Action," *Industry Week* (CompuServe online edition), November 4, 1996.
6. Chris Marshall, Larry Prusak, and David Shpilberg, "Financial Risk

and the Need for Superior Knowledge Management," *California Management Review*, Spring 1996, pp. 77(25).

7. Kinni, op. cit.
8. David Bank, "Know-It-Alls," *Wall Street Journal*, November 18, 1996, p. R28.

6

The Knowledge Network: Building Support for Employee and Organizational Learning

Knowledge is of two kinds. We know a subject ourselves, or we know where we can find information upon it.

Samuel Johnson (1709–1784)

Many companies today want to become knowledge-enabled organizations to ensure that all employees are able to locate, access, and utilize the knowledge and skills they need to meet their individual and company goals. Through the learning contract, employees identify their learning needs. The knowledge network provides the means to organize, store, and give access to the collective knowledge of all company employees. Where the needed knowledge and skills cannot be represented electronically in a database, the knowledge network offers pointers and access to learning resources.

Why is the knowledge network so important to the knowledge-enabled organization? Arthur Andersen's Robert J. Hiebeler answers this way:

> Access to organizational knowledge has become more critical to achieving and sustaining competitive advantage than the knowledge that individual members possess. Professionals can no longer know everything they need to do their jobs well. They have to be able to get to critical information—fast—whenever and wherever they need it. In the future, organizations that are able to provide their members with rapid access to the full repository of organizational knowledge are the organizations that are most likely to succeed.[1]

This chapter presents some excellent practices that companies have undertaken to build their own knowledge networks; it is a guide for starting to build your company's knowledge network.

The Major Components of a Knowledge Network

Please note: This discussion is not on specific technical components, such as computers or telecommunications networks, although these are necessary to building a knowledge network. We do not discuss specific technologies here because they change so fast that technical information current at the time of writing is already out-of-date. Your company should work with its own information services organization or provider to determine the best technological solution to provide these capabilities.

There are four major components to a knowledge network:

1. A repository, most commonly a computerized database, of specific company knowledge and experience
2. A directory of the specific knowledge, skills, and experience held by groups and individual employees throughout the company

3. A directory of learning resources, within and without the company, that employees can access to help them plan their own learning activities
4. A set of tools, methods, and capabilities that enable employees to learn from each other and to learn together

The Repository of Company Knowledge

Some of the earliest attempts at managing knowledge came as companies developed call centers to answer their customers' questions. Within an active customer call center, operators continuously field questions about the company's products and services. Without a plan to categorize common questions and answers, each operator would have to develop a new answer to each question. The result would be a great waste of time and effort, with inconsistent answers to a given question among different operators.

Butterball Turkey has been at this business for more than sixteen years, with a hotline that consumers can call to ask questions about purchasing and preparing turkeys for their holiday meals. According to Carol Miller, a supervisor at the hotline, Butterball receives two hundred thousand calls per year, with common questions ranging from selecting the right size turkey to how to thaw a frozen turkey to how to save a burning turkey.

Miller says Butterball has been in business for more than forty years and has developed extensive knowledge from work in its test kitchens over that period. This knowledge was organized first into manuals and later into a database accessible by the home economists who answer consumer calls. Potential questions are classified into almost seventy different categories that can be accessed through the operators' computer terminals, in the paper-based manual, and now from Butterball's home page on the Internet. These categories cover virtually every question a customer can ask (although a few new questions and answers are added every year).

By organizing its collective knowledge, Butterball simplifies the job of its home economists, ensures that consumers get the right answer each time, and makes the process much more cost effective than if the database did not exist. Other companies with such customer hotlines—from computer companies to consumer product companies, from government agencies to health care organizations—have developed similar question-and-answer databases for the same reasons.

Another well-known example of a knowledge repository is Dow Chemical's database of patents, trademarks, and copyrights, described in Chapter 3. Buckman Laboratories, discussed in Chapter 2, has created knowledge databases covering its products, services, and applications categorized by industry (paper-making, agriculture, etc.). Ernst & Young has a series of eighty "power packs," or "databases containing information on particular areas of the firm's practice, such as expatriate tax processing or changing regulations in the health industry."[2] Ford Motor Company's knowledge repositories include such data as "detail blueprints of rival vehicles, engineering methods for problems such as door closures, corporate-approved design styles, and specs for hundreds of thousands of parts."[3]

Dow has extended its database beyond patent information to include company "know-how": the nonpatented but vital manufacturing processes, engineering tools, and other business practices developed within the company over the years. Too often, employees in one part of a company spend large amounts of time, effort, and money developing a new business practice or a new technology only to discover later that the work has already been done, or the investment already made, in another part of the company.

When the Canadian Imperial Bank of Commerce (CIBC) developed an inventory of external training programs and licenses owned by the bank (an effort that took six months), they found that they owned sixteen different training programs on a single word processing system—and that three different groups within the bank had purchased nationwide licenses for the same management training program. Had CIBC placed information on programs and licenses owned by the bank in a knowledge repository, it could have avoided these costly duplications.

A company's knowledge repository should comprise:

* Basic company information, including public relations information, annual reports, press releases, company overview presentations, etc.

* Information about organization, including a directory of locations, agents, distributors, service centers, etc.
* Information about its products and services, including sales literature and technical specifications
* Information about basic business processes
* Information about patents, trademarks, copyrights, and licenses to use other companies' technologies, programs, and processes
* Customer information

One way of determining the information that should reside in the repository is to examine the cumulative learning needs of company employees, as specified in their learning contracts. What information do employees say they need to find to get their jobs done? Would including that information in the knowledge repository help employees accomplish their learning and their business goals more efficiently?

A knowledge repository organizes, and makes available to all employees, basic information on the company's organization, products, services, customers, and business processes.

The knowledge in the repository must be what employees need, but it is not limited to knowledge generated within the company. Many businesses place information about competitors and their products and services in the database. This information may be generated by the company's own competitive analysis department or purchased from outside industry watchers. According to Chief Knowledge Officer Dave Pollard, Ernst & Young of Canada assesses the value and negotiates the purchase price of a wide variety of external databases to include in its knowledge repository. These external resources contain information on such topics as "company information, industry analyses, financial benchmarks, leading practices, regulatory information, newsfeeds, and specialized online periodicals."

The types of information in the preceding list are explicit knowledge, easily represented in words and data. Much of this information already exists on paper, in company publications or reports, but distribution of the documents is so limited that they never reach the people who could really use them. But much of the knowledge held by employees is tacit in nature, coming more from experience than from facts.

Some companies have made great efforts to transform at least some of this tacit knowledge into explicit knowledge. Buckman Laboratories has assembled a set of almost twenty-five hundred case studies, which Buckman's John Burrows defined for me as "an electronic copy recording how a front-line sales associate created new knowledge within our organization . . . by resolving a problem at their customer's business either by applying existing 'Buckman knowledge' if it was a new problem or by developing a new, more effective or efficient solution if it was a well-documented problem." All of these case studies, some dating back to 1988, are available from the Buckman knowledge repository, K'Netix®, The Buckman Knowledge Network™.

Guidelines for a Good Knowledge Network

Whatever form your company's knowledge repository takes— and there are many technology options for building such a repository—here are a few basic guidelines for giving your employees a useful and used tool:

* *Organize the database and keep it useful.* Many computers are filled with useless and unused data. The people who built the applications that created many of today's large databases may no longer be associated with them, and use and effectiveness are often not measured at all. If you want the knowledge repository to be used as a learning tool, it must be well organized, kept up-to-date, and easy to access and search. If it is too difficult for employees to find what they need in the repository, they either find other ways to discover the information they need to do their jobs more effectively and efficiently—or, worse, they go without. Later in this chapter, we discuss the tasks involved in maintaining the repository and other parts of the knowledge network.

* *Keep the information in the database accurate.* With some

databases, once data enter they never leave—even when outdated or replaced by more accurate information. Ensure that when employees get information from the repository, they can rely on its accuracy and timeliness. It doesn't take many instances of an employee finding inaccurate data before he questions the accuracy of all the data and therefore stops using the repository.

＊ *Give all employees direct access to the repository.* While certain sections may require passwords or other security measures because of the sensitivity of the data, no employee should have to go through an approval process to gain access to the information she needs to do her job. Requiring such approvals obviates the principles of just-in-time learning.

＊ *Provide easy-access tools for all employees.* The Silicon Graphics knowledge network has grown so large that the company created a "gateway" to "help integrate [its many components] and give employees easier access to information throughout the organization." The gateway "now offers an easy-to-use index of news, employee services, product and sales information, as well as customer and technical support information. It includes sophisticated search tools that enable the user to quickly access desired information."[4]

The repository may contain all of the needed explicit knowledge within the company, and many companies attempt to include some types of tacit knowledge. But there are always other types of tacit knowledge, along with actual skills, that cannot be captured in the repository, for they exist only in the employees' heads. When an employee needs to find tacit knowledge or skills held by other employees, he does not rely on the knowledge repository, but on a *directory* of knowledge, skills, and experience held by groups and individual employees.

The Directory of Knowledge, Skills, and Experience

Although many companies have sophisticated inventory systems in place to keep track of their stocks of physical assets (raw materials, parts, finished goods, etc.), few keep any inventory of their knowledge and skill assets. The few exceptions have sophisticated systems that track specific job-related competencies, often in the manufacturing arena (as Caterpillar does for its factory employees) or where competency systems are mandated by government regulators, as in the nuclear power industry. Some companies, such as GE, have created databases on best practices from their various business units (as we saw in Chapter 5). Arthur Andersen's Global Best Practices℠ knowledge base "captures best practices from external and internal sources and [uses] CD-ROM technology to share that information throughout the company."[5]

The directory of knowledge, skills, and experience is a vehicle for keeping track of human assets. More than a resume database, it provides information on every company employee, regardless of level, function, or location, and may include such data as:

* Education: degrees, majors and minors, company courses completed, specific continuing education courses, etc.
* Experience: jobs held, companies worked for, types of work done, methods used (e.g., total quality management, statistical process control, process modeling), and fields of expertise, experience, and interest, whether or not they relate to the employee's current job.
* Competencies achieved (whether section is supported by a formal competency database or not): specific competencies related to current job as well as any area in which the company works; technical skills and "softer" skills such as meeting facilitation, team management, etc.

Suppose an employee requires a particular skill to complete a given assignment. If the skill is needed on a long-term basis, the employee includes it in her learning contract as an area for development. If, on the other hand, the skill is needed for a short period of time to complete just one project, she might use the directory to find another employee who can contribute the skill ad hoc.

Consulting companies such as Ernst & Young and Arthur

Andersen use these directory capabilities to assemble project teams. Dave Pollard says that Ernst & Young of Canada "is working to incorporate both competency/skill information and schedule information, for our employees, in a single knowledge base, so that we can identify not only who has the needed skills but also who is available."

Andersen Worldwide uses directory listings as part of its knowledge network, known as ANet, "to self-organize instantly around a customer's problem anywhere in the world. ANet thus taps into otherwise dormant capabilities and expands the energies and solution sets available to customers."[6]

Directory databases also enable employees to create what Xerox's John Seeley Brown calls "communities of interest": groups of people scattered throughout the company who have a common interest in a technology, industry, product, or other area, who, although not working together on any specific project, communicate informally to build knowledge for the company and themselves.

The directory is also useful to employees searching for learning resources—that is, people—to help fulfill their learning contracts. They can search for other people with knowledge or experience in their area of interest. This is especially important to the sharing of tacit knowledge, which is primarily communicated person-to-person. These learning resource people can then offer suggestions for reading, courses, or other developmental experiences; mentor or coach the employee through learning activities; or simply spend some time talking with the employee to share their knowledge and answer questions.

The Directory of Learning Resources

The knowledge network includes both a learning resources database and a library of learning materials. The learning resources database contains data on learning opportunities that may encompass:

* The company's training catalog and schedule of formal training programs.

* A listing of self-paced learning materials (paper-,

media-, and computer-based) available within the company, as well as instructions on how to sign up for a course or order materials.

✳ Listings of, and pointers to, external learning opportunities, such as courses, workshops, conferences, and symposia offered by colleges and universities, professional societies, consultants, and professional seminar companies. The opportunities may also include satellite courses, audio- and videotapes, books, computer-based instruction, etc.

✳ Complete listings of the company's library as well as links to other libraries. Today, it is possible to have live links to news services and indexes of business and professional literature—including full text and graphics retrieval capabilities—from the employee's desktop personal computer. Some companies give their employees full access to the World Wide Web. (Some others, of course, restrict access or use of the Web to discourage employees from wasting time.)

It is also possible to structure this database so that employees can add their comments on and reactions to specific programs they have attended. At a minimum, they can attach the names and locations of company employees who have attended specific programs or used specific learning materials, so that others can get a personal reference on the program's usefulness.

The directory of learning resources is of particular value to employees as they plan their learning contracts. A fully implemented directory can provide employees with a number of alternative learning sources and methods for most of the learning needs specified in their contracts.

Sun Microsystems has one of the best online directories of learning resources I have seen; it includes most of the capabilities specified above. Other companies such as CIBC and PPG Industries provide excellent paper-based learning guides that contain pointers to company-sponsored courses and self-study materials.

Learning and Management Tools

The knowledge network also contains a number of tools and methods for employees to communicate with each other. More than just e-mail, these capabilities include group-specific and open discussion forums, management tools, and groupware capabilities through which employees can more effectively work and learn together and from each other.

K'Netix®, The Buckman Knowledge Network™, includes several discussion forums through which any employee can ask a question and receive answers from others (including the chairman). The beauty of these forums is that the person asking the question is often amazed to find out who can answer it. This knowledge-sharing application thus makes it possible for any Buckman employee to take advantage of the knowledge and skills of other employees, including those outside her workgroup, business unit, or location.

Similar capabilities serve Andersen specialists: "by posting problems on electronic bulletin boards and following up with visual and data contacts [they can] self-organize instantly around a customer's problem anywhere in the world."[7] At Wunderman Cato Johnsons in New York City, a subsidiary of the Young & Rubicam advertising agency, these tools "help people working with the same client in different countries to brainstorm better advertising," says Chief Knowledge Officer Nicholas Rudd.[8] Some companies allow customers and suppliers to participate in interactive discussion, while others restrict them to special forums designed for interaction with employees.

Computer-based work tools on the knowledge network allow employees to collaborate across time and distance. In some companies, work is passed around the globe as working hours end in one location and start in another. Another example of such collaboration comes from Ford, where

> Emil Sims, a 25-year-old suspension engineer, is developing an all-new light truck from his desktop in Dearborn, the center of Ford's light-truck efforts. But because his vehicle is also a front-wheel-drive model, Mr. Sims often uses his workstation to work with colleagues in Europe, the home of Ford's vehicle-development center for front-wheel-drive small cars.[9]

There may be some generic tools that employees can utilize to create their own working and learning groups, but your company may also want to customize applications to support your specific business. Michael Saylor of MicroStrategy, Inc., gives several examples of this type of application:

> A bank can rise above its competition by providing decision support software that analyzes receipts from customers, payments to suppliers, and asset flows. Health insurance companies can strengthen the loyalty of a corporate client by providing better expense reporting and therapeutic treatment statistics for area caregivers. A travel agency can provide a system to control costs, analyze business travel patterns, and centrally manage a worldwide travel policy.[10]

Through such applications, companies provide their own employees and their customers with the knowledge they need to do their jobs better.

The knowledge network can be enabled and facilitated by technology, but the real key is giving people the *information* they need to succeed. In a conference handout titled "Hughes Space & Communications' Knowledge Highway," Arian Ward stresses that the technologies are secondary to the act of sharing knowledge: "HSC's Knowledge Highway (KH) [is] about people and tapping their knowledge and potential. It's about linking them so they can share their knowledge and learn from each other. It's about becoming enlightened to the unlimited possibilities that these intellectual assets offer."

Building Your Company's Knowledge Network

Companies that want to build their own knowledge networks should work with their information systems and telecommunications groups or vendors to discuss the best technological solutions. This section focuses instead on how to organize people to build and maintain the content of the knowledge network.

Building the Knowledge Repository

When starting to build a knowledge repository, companies are well advised to deliberate on what information belongs in it. It is all too easy to say "Let's put in everything we have"—especially with today's technical capabilities to easily scan documents into a database. What you want is not all of the information you have, but a structured set of data and documents that contain the information employees need to get their jobs done. This information should be well organized and indexed by both general areas of interest and keywords that make it easy for employees to search the database for information on any topic. Full-text search capability also facilitates the process.

Successful companies start with a team of expert knowledge resources (people) to determine what should reside in each section of the knowledge database.

﹡ Dow began with cross-disciplinary groups called "intellectual asset management teams" to identify key technology know-how. "The teams are asking what information is key, where it resides, and how it's articulated," says Gordon Petrash. "They are finding out who keeps what knowledge and what the associated patents are. They're figuring out where knowledge fits into the process. They're setting parameters."[11]

﹡ Harris Corp. appoints individuals as "certified practice experts" and gives those individuals responsibility for content.

﹡ CKO Pollard at Ernst & Young of Canada uses the term *knowledge network* to refer to "the team of people (internal and external) who share knowledge and expertise in a particular subject area."

﹡ Boeing gives responsibility for each knowledge management section to whichever team is in charge of designing that portion of the aircraft (tail, ailerons, fuselage, etc.).[12]

﹡ Buckman Laboratories appoints "section leaders," who have responsibility to build and maintain the content of each section of the knowledge repository and the associated forums. The section leaders are knowledgeable about the topics contained in the section and are also responsible for calling in whatever expert resources they need to help them with the task.

It is important that these groups of experts not only rely on their own knowledge but also ask the advice of the people who will be using the knowledge network. A high-powered group of headquarters personnel, told to create a knowledge database (or a training program or manual) for field personnel, could go about their task without ever consulting the target audience. Not only is this practice arrogant, but it also means that the field personnel the database is being designed for will view it as "theirs" rather than "ours." It also implies a database designed according to the needs and wishes of the headquarters group, rather than those of its eventual users.

To get people started using the knowledge repository, it is important that the company not just announce its availability and provide instruction sheets for use. Training sessions, demonstrations, contests, and other promotional events get people interested in the repository. When a support group, or a member of the team that built the repository, receives a phone call or mail message asking for information that resides within the repository, the caller should be pointed to the repository even if it is easier to just answer the question orally. If necessary, the caller should be walked through how to find the answer in the repository (even if the caller has already received the instruction sheet or attended a training session). The idea is to change employees' habits, to get them used to the new way of finding the information they need. Chapter 7 presents more ideas on this topic.

Building the Directory of Knowledge, Skills, and Experience

The four steps to building the directory of knowledge, skills, and experience are:

1. Selecting an easy-to-use, easy-to-maintain, easy-to-access database technology with the assistance of your company's information services group or provider. A good beginning is to

develop a competency database, resume database, or other type of human resources information system (HRIS).

2. Defining the key variables to be included in the directory. The variables should be the same for every employee. Many companies are surprised to find that employees in one function have capabilities associated with those of a different function as a result of prior education or work experience. The idea of the database is to cover every capability of every employee, regardless of level, function, or location.

3. Getting employees to enter their own data. Employees must be mandated to complete their profiles. Some employees decline to do so because of modesty, because they're overqualified for their current positions and don't want it known, or because they fear being inundated with requests for help if they include particular skills that are in great demand but short supply.

4. Getting employees to use the directory. Employees must also be encouraged to use it—as a learning resource. They might fear that asking someone else for help exposes their own ignorance and results in poor performance evaluations. We need to get beyond that mentality, to the point where we reward employees for getting a problem solved no matter what the source of the solution. Getting employees to use the database may also require communication about its importance and training on how to use it.

Who should be in charge of the database? The logical choice is the human resources group, since it is likely to have responsibility for any existing competency or HRIS databases.

The Directory of Learning Resources

This database should be built and managed by the training and development (T&D) or human resources development (HRD) group. As stated earlier, the library and training catalog form the starting point for this database, and the T&D/HRD group typically has responsibility for those two items.

The directory should also include notices of college and university courses, professional society workshops, satellite courses available to the company, local workshops, etc. Some employees already receive notices of programs as members of professional associations or subscribers to industry or professional magazines. But these notices rarely circulate beyond the individual or the individual's group. Entering program information into the directory of learning resources gives all employees access to it.

As with all of the databases and directories being discussed here, ensure that the information is organized effectively, easily searched by keywords or through full text, and kept current. Chapter 8 emphasizes that these responsibilities fit well with the newly defined role of employee and organizational learning for the training/HRD group.

Learning and Management Tools

These include basic communications technologies (e-mail, teleconferencing, video conferencing, etc.) along with a variety of tools most commonly called "groupware." Floyd Kemske, editor of *CBT Solutions,* lists the following categories of support structures used in what he calls electronic performance support systems:

* Searchable reference
* Explanations
* Context-sensitive help
* Demonstrations
* Tool tips
* Interactive instruction
* Context-independent help
* Task guides, wizards, or coaches
* Application tours
* Cue cards
* Screen tours[13]

Although these relate most specifically to supporting the use of system-based tools and applications, they can all be reasonably included in this category of learning and management tools.

A key application for individual and organizational learning is the discussion forum. There are a number of software products available to build discussion forums. Rather than build its own network and develop its own software capabilities, Buckman Laboratories opted to sign on with CompuServe and build private forums there for Buckman employees.

Starting discussion forums involves more than just assigning topic names to various sections. Buckman assigned system operators ("sysops") to handle the systems end of the forums and "section leaders" to handle the technical content of the questions submitted to the forums and the answers provided. A section leader has to be someone interested in the subject of the forum and well connected within the company, at least with regard to the subject matter. When an employee submits a question to the forum, the section leader:

* Works with the employee to clarify any unclear question.
* Finds someone to get the question (and any answers to the question) translated if the question is written in a language other than English (or the company's primary language). This requirement is increasingly important as companies become global enterprises and have many employees in foreign countries.
* Ensures that responses offered by other employees are correct and fit with company policies and practices.
* Makes corrections and ensures that the questioner does not act on incorrect information.
* Finds a knowledgeable person if no one responds to the question.
* Provides pointers to any answer that resides in the knowledge repository or forum libraries.

Maintaining Forums, Libraries, and Databases

A knowledge network will be used only if employees find it easy to use and its contents accurate and up to date.

Interactive forums tend to get very busy—and cumbersome if completed question-and-answer segments are not "harvested" to make room for new crops. The metaphor is apt, because the section leader takes each question and associated responses, separates the wheat from the chaff, bundles the wheat into a tight package, and places it in the forum library. The library is organized by the same topic areas as the forum itself and is indexed by keywords to make it easy to search.

An important next step—one that few companies undertake—is to manage the forum libraries, which tend to become very large and very quickly disorganized. The libraries should be examined, at least quarterly, and reorganized to condense their contents, group similar topics together, etc. If the library contains new and stable knowledge—as examples, a new application of an existing product that is now generally accepted, or a procedure for fixing a problem with a new product—that information should be moved to the knowledge repository. The entry in the forum library should then be replaced, at least temporarily, with a pointer to the new section in the knowledge repository.

Over time, some of the library sections go out-of-date: The recommended solution to a customer's problem from two years ago may have been replaced by a new product or service. When this happens, the library section needs to be eliminated or at least changed to reflect current solutions.

If repeated questions in the forum point to a problem with a product, an error in the product manual, or an aspect of a service that people don't seem to understand, the section leader must relay this information to the appropriate group. For example, the training group might need to add a topic to an existing training program, or the technical writing group may have to update a manual, or the product engineers may have to modify the product.

Who should be in charge of this set of learning and management tools? The information services and communications groups within the company can take responsibility for building or buying the needed applications. The content of the applications belongs to the people who have the knowledge: the group of experts who define the contents of the databases, the section leaders who control the discussion forums, and the teams or other groups who use the tools to help manage their work and facilitate individual and group learning.

Making Groupware Work

All the technology and capabilities of a knowledge network can *enable* a company's employees to work together, that is, make it possible. They can also *facilitate* the employees working together, that is, make it easy. But no technology can *make* people work together. Barbara Mroz of Nika*Interactive,* a consultancy based in Greenfield, Massachusetts, has identified "twelve managerial issues which managers must address in order to get the highest performance from groups using electronic collaboration."[14]

1. The business purpose is clear.
2. Sponsors walk the talk.
3. Project resources are stable.
4. The host organization is hospitable.
5. The group has collaborative characteristics.
6. The group share a common sense of purpose.
7. The group communicates both formally and informally.
8. Collaboration tools are matched to tasks.
9. The effects of electronic communication are managed.
10. The changing group dynamics are managed.
11. The group collaboration is monitored.
12. Progress is communicated.

Let's examine each of these managerial issues with respect to the knowledge network.

A Clear Business Purpose

The primary purpose of the knowledge-enabled organization and all its component parts, including the knowledge network, is to help employees and the company succeed. If the company does not have clear goals, and if employees do not view the knowledge network as a valuable tool in achieving their goals, they will not use it, no matter how good it is or how easy it is to use.

Walking the Talk

Leaders must lead by example. If leaders want employees to use the knowledge network, they must use it themselves. Bob Buckman, chairman of Buckman Laboratories, is perhaps the most constant user of the company's knowledge network. Through his personal use, he is demonstrating not only the network's importance to the company's business, but also his own willingness to act as a learning resource for other company employees.

Stable Project Resources

Building and maintaining a knowledge network requires substantial resources—money, time, and personnel. It is not a short-term project, but a long-term commitment to changing the way in which company employees work. Nothing will kill a knowledge-enabled organization faster than building a knowledge network and then suddenly pulling support from it and letting it waste away. Resources for building and maintaining the network must be stable.

A Hospitable Host Organization

A knowledge network cannot survive in an organization whose culture prohibits or discourages communication and collaboration. It can thrive only when the company has built a positive learning environment, as will be described in Chapter 7.

Collaborative Characteristics Within the Group

The use of groupware to facilitate collaboration happens faster if groups have been collaborating before the introduction of the knowledge network. In this case, the new tools will serve only to help groups get their work done more efficiently. If the company culture had previously discouraged collaboration, then groupware, no matter how good, will not make it happen. Open communication and the sharing of goals and resources—elements of a positive learning environment—are what make the eventual success of the knowledge network more certain.

A Common Sense of Purpose

According to Barbara Mroz, "Group members must understand and believe in the purpose for electronic collaboration. They have to internalize the importance of using it and have common expectations for its results."[15]

Communication Both Formally and Informally

Collaboration, whether or not it is supported electronically, works best when group members have both personal and professional relationships. A study of a concurrent engineering project, where team members were scattered across the United States and Europe, concluded that by bringing the group together for an initial period, team members were able to establish personal as well as professional affiliations that did a great deal to improve the group's cohesiveness and business results as members worked together electronically over great distances. Informal personal communications among group members, whether electronically or in person, are vital to a group's success.

Collaboration Tools Matched to Tasks

The numbers and types of tools under the banner of groupware increase every day. Some are better for certain forms of work than others. Mroz states: "Electronic meeting systems, for instance, can be effective in group brainstorming and prioritizing but are not as effective for project management. Using electronic mail to negotiate can make the process of reaching agreement more difficult and more time-consuming. Managers must know which tools to use and when to use them."[16]

Managing the Effects of Electronic Communications

Early users of electronic mail learned some hard lessons about when and when not to use e-mail. Electronic communications generally cannot convey tone of voice or body language. People sometimes send out very hostile messages in the heat of the moment when they would normally have calmed down before attending a meeting on the subject hours or days later. Some companies even made incredibly egregious errors, such as sending termination notices to employees by e-mail. The effects of electronic communications must be understood and managed, or they will not succeed.

For example, e-mail makes it easy to get into what are known as "memo wars." It starts when person A receives an e-mail message from person B that angers him. He quickly writes a hostile reply and, in sending it by e-mail, decides that it would be very easy to send a copy to B's manager. When B reads this hostile response, and sees that his manager was copied, he writes an even nastier reply, copies his own manager, and sends copies to A, A's manager, and the rest of A's group. As these "wars" continue, the list of people getting copies of the messages keeps growing, until there is no hope of ever salvaging the situation between A and B, their managers, or their groups. E-mail distribution lists can be a great time-saver, but their ease of use can also have unintended results, as with memo wars.

Monitoring and Managing Changing Group Dynamics

Electronic communications level the playing field. Power relationships are less evident. Bob Buckman's message on the knowledge network is just another message, not "an official communication from the chairman." Mroz states: "More people may participate in discussions than before, the balance of power may shift away from those who hold sway in person-to-person meetings, and conflicts can easily get out of hand electronically. Managers must understand these effects up front, and create constructive mechanisms to keep the group on track."[17]

Monitoring the Group Collaboration Process

Managers need to monitor the use of the knowledge network to ensure that it is being used correctly and productively. If some groups of employees are not, for whatever reason, participating fully in the knowledge network, they will not be helped by the network to improve individual job performance or to share their own knowledge and skills with others who might find them of value. Managers need to monitor these types of behavioral cues and take appropriate action to correct undesirable behaviors. Also, electronic communications can and should be used to build and maintain personal relationships among employees in remote locations, but this usage should not be the primary function of the network.

Communicating Progress

Nothing will increase participation in the knowledge network more than stories of individual and company success (new business won, unnecessary costs avoided, new ideas generated, and so forth) based on its use. Communicating success encourages employees to use the network to help ensure their own success.

Conclusion: Building a Supportive Knowledge Network

No matter how technically sophisticated the knowledge network, it does not add any value or enable the company to become a knowledge-enabled organization unless employees at all levels use it. Some of the ideas in this chapter have focused on making this set of tools easy to use. More important is creating a positive learning environment throughout all levels, functions, and locations of the company. Without a positive learning environment, no organization can become knowledge-enabled, regardless of how much it spends on tools and technologies. In the next chapter, we discuss how today's successful companies create a positive learning environment.

Notes

1. Robert J. Hiebeler, "The Value of Sharing Best Practices," conference handout, 1995.
2. David Bank, "Know-It-Alls," *Wall Street Journal*, November 18, 1996, p. R28. Reprinted by permission of *The Wall Street Journal* © 1996 Dow Jones & Company, Inc. All rights reserved worldwide.
3. Oscar Suris, "Behind the Wheel," *Wall Street Journal*, November 18, 1996, p. R14. Reprinted by permission of *The Wall Street Journal* © 1996 Dow Jones & Company, Inc. All rights reserved worldwide.
4. Britton Manasco, "Silicon Graphics Develops Powerful Knowledge Network," *Knowledge, Inc.*, January 1997, p. 2.
5. Robert J. Hiebeler, "Benchmarking Knowledge Management," *Strategy & Leadership*, March–April 1996, pp. 22–28.
6. James B. Quinn, Philip Anderson, and Sydney Finkelstein, "Managing Professional Intellect: Making the Most of the Best," *Harvard Business Review*, March–April 1996, p. 76.
7. Ibid.
8. Laura B. Smith, "The Thinkers," *PC Week*, August 5, 1996, pp. 1–2.
9. Suris, op. cit., p. 76.
10. Michael Saylor, "Decision Support on the Web," *Knowledge, Inc.*, January 1997, p. 7.
11. Rick Mullin, "Knowledge Management: A Cultural Evolution," *Journal of Business Strategy*, September–October 1996, pp. 56–59.
12. Marcelo Hoffmann and Kermit M. Patton, "Knowledge Empowers Boeing, Verifone, and Chaparral Steel," *Knowledge, Inc.*, December 1996.
13. Floyd Kemske, "Mid-Morning After the Dawn of EPSS," *CBT Solutions*, September–October 1996, p. 8.
14. Barbara Mroz, "Making Electronic Collaboration Work" (Greenfield, Mass.: NIKA*Interactive*, 1997).
15. Ibid., p. 3.
16. Ibid., pp. 3–4.
17. Ibid., p. 4.

7

Fostering a Positive Learning Environment

Personally, I'm always ready to learn, although I
do not always like being taught.

Winston Churchill

To succeed in becoming a knowledge-enabled organization, a
company must change how the leaders lead; how it structures
communications, up, down, and throughout the company; how
it measures and rewards employees; and how it structures work
and designs jobs. Simply investing in training programs or information technology or production machinery is not enough. Successful change efforts depend on many concurrent activities and
investments. Economists call this concept "complementarity."

Complementarity and Measures of Worth

If learning activities are properly designed, and knowledge and
skills are developed, how do you measure their worth? Suppose
two work groups attend the same training program. If the manager of group A feels the topic of training is worthwhile and
follows up the training by coaching her employees and reinforc-
ing their learning, group A may reap substantial benefits from
the training. If the manager of group B does not believe that

the training program is worthwhile and sends his group to the program only because it has been mandated from above, he will not reinforce the learning or coach the employees. In fact, manager B may tell employees to forget what they learned, that he expects them to continue doing their work in the old way; there will be no return on the investment in the training program. So what is the value of the training?

Similarly, if you invest in information technology, how do you measure its effects on the organization and changes in productivity? If you reorganize the corporation, how do you measure the benefits of the new organization? The value of any of these investments comes from how they are used. In writing about the benefits of technology, Stanford University's Nathan Rosenberg states that

> . . . economic impact is not something that can be extrapolated out of a piece of hardware. New technologies, rather, need to be conceived as building blocks. Their eventual impact will depend on what is subsequently designed and constructed with them. New technologies are unrealized potentials that may take a very large number of eventual shapes. What shapes they actually take will depend on the ability to visualize how they might be employed *in new contexts*."[1]

Just as technology is one type of "building block," so are knowledge and skills. Their value is not inherent but comes only from application. Summarizing the findings of a 1996 conference on technology and growth sponsored by the Federal Reserve Bank of Boston, Bennett Harrison said:

> The answer [to technology's effect on economic growth] . . . centered on a notion now hotly discussed by economists, called "complementarity." Simply put, investments in production technologies cannot achieve their potential without a number of concurrent developments. These might include the introduction of more flexible workplace organizations, the delegation of greater responsibility to nonmanagerial labor, the en-

hancement of skills among both managers and their employees, and the installation of new infrastructure, ranging from Internet connections to new-fashioned airports to "smart," energy-efficient buildings.[2]

Because of this notion of complementarity, it becomes virtually impossible to identify the benefits of any single component of the company's transformation effort. Evaluation can only be macro, at the level of the company's balance sheet and income statement. How much have we invested in the overall transformation program? Have these investments enabled the company to meet its goals, in terms of return on stockholder equity and other financial measures? in terms of market share? the targets set in the company's vision statement?

Changes in learning methods must be complemented by strong leadership, flexible organizations, and supportive policies and procedures if the knowledge-enabled organization is to succeed.

Becoming a knowledge-enabled organization isn't really a choice for companies that are trying to build a strong future. Over the past decade, many companies facing tough economic times have opted to "slash and burn," downsizing their operations and making massive cuts in personnel to respond to poor performance. Downsizing has not proved to be an effective strategy for most companies because they have done little to change how work is done, other than to require those remaining to continue to do business in the same old ways but with fewer people and resources. According to AlliedSignal's Lawrence Bossidy,

> Well, the smoke has started to clear, and for some companies, things look pretty much the same as they did before.
>
> ✴ Some haven't revamped their processes to prevent defects which increase the costs of scrap, rework, and inspection.
> ✴ They haven't analyzed their operations to root out unnec-

essary work that adds no value in the eye of the customer.

* They haven't benchmarked other companies to find a better way of doing things or even spread best practices within their own company.
* They haven't eliminated duplicative administrative functions by setting up centers of excellence which perform repetitive, high-volume, transactional functions for the entire enterprise.

In short, they used to live in a big messy house, and now they live in a small messy house.[3]

Companies like Buckman Laboratories and many others featured throughout this book are well on their way to becoming knowledge-enabled organizations. They have one thing in common: Their CEOs all have an unshakable belief that these programs are absolutely vital to the company's future. These CEOs see no choice but to implement the full array of programs and changes that constitute the knowledge-enabled organization, and they have full faith that the results of today's investments will show up in future balance sheets and income statements.

But if we can only judge the overall benefits of the knowledge-enabled organization on the basis of macro measurements, then how do we make wise decisions and evaluate them regarding individual components of the transformation effort, individual training programs, investments in information technology, and the changes in job design and the other factors that complement what is recommended in this book?

For many years, I have argued that there are three primary questions to ask in evaluating any learning intervention (be that a training program, a knowledge network, a change in organizational design, or any other type):

1. Relevance: Do the people who participate in or are affected by the intervention feel that the changes are relevant to their goals? We often design programs or other interventions and then force people to participate when they have no idea how they relate to work and goals.
2. Value: Do the people who are designated as the benefi-

ciaries of the learning activity feel that it adds value to their work? If not, why conduct the activity?

3. Quality: Is the learning activity a high-quality effort? (The traditional measures for evaluating training programs and other activities are whether the materials are clear, the instructor is knowledgeable, and the facilities are comfortable.)

This chapter examines some basic ways in which a company can create a positive learning environment—a prime prerequisite to the knowledge-enabled organization. The path to continuous improvement is continuous learning, and continuous learning does not take place in an environment where learning is not valued. Each component of a positive learning environment complements the others, that is, they are all required and must all work together to create the learning environment needed to build a knowledge-enabled organization.

Microsoft's Continuous Learning Culture

A prime example of a company built on continuous learning is Microsoft, one of the great success stories in twentieth-century American business. Reflecting on the lessons learned from their examination of the Microsoft culture, Michael Cusumano and Richard Selby write:

> Organizations have many opportunities to improve whatever it is that they do: They can reflect on their operations, study their products, listen to customers, and encourage different parts of the organization to share knowledge as well as the results of their separate efforts, such as in designing products and components. All firms have these opportunities, although few companies take full advantage of them.[4]

Microsoft was built on the principles of knowledge sharing and creation. Its culture and learning environment focus more on knowledge sharing than on formal training. The same authors report that

Rather than investing heavily in training programs, formal rules and procedures, or even detailed product documentation, Microsoft tries to hire people who can learn on their own on the job. It then relies on experienced people to educate and guide new people: Team leads, experts in certain areas, and formally appointed mentors take on the burden of teaching in addition to their own work.[5]

But for most companies, creating a knowledge-enabled organization is a major cultural shift, and, like any other cultural change, it cannot succeed without strong, committed, visible leadership.

Leadership for Learning

Does your company's CEO value learning and sharing knowledge? Does he or she participate in learning activities, for his or her own learning and to share knowledge with employees?

✳ General Electric's Jack Welch is a frequent participant in the company's programs at its Crotonville, New York, center. He has personally led dozens of "WorkOut!" sessions at company facilities, where frontline workers share their ideas and suggestions for improvements—ideas that mostly have been rejected or ignored by their own managers.

✳ A member of Amoco's executive committee spends half a day per week, forty weeks per year, participating in programs at the Amoco Management Learning Center, sharing his views with managers from throughout the company and learning their views and concerns.

✳ Skandia, the large Swedish financial services company, created the Skandia Future Centers, a team of thirty hand-picked people from around the world, to explore the driving forces of the business environment and "to present a vision of the future to Skandia's corporate council, the company's 150 senior executives."[6]

✳ Merck & Co. CEO Raymond Gilmartin says that the way he operates is "to be receptive to other people's ideas and to basically respect what they do. I get a lot in return." In the same vein, he "pushes staffers to air problems and debate without regard for hierarchy—and without getting personal."[7]

Leaders can inspire and empower employees at all levels to use their own knowledge, share that knowledge, innovate, and solve the "insoluble" problems that plague every company. According to Ranganath Nayak, senior vice-president of Arthur D. Little, "Senior executives are increasingly accepting their role in leading change and recognizing the amount of knowledge resident in their people. Employee knowledge can't be boiled down into a process; it has to be nurtured, shared, and captured."[8]

But leaders cannot build a positive learning environment by sitting in their corner offices high atop corporate headquarters and issuing an occasional memo. It takes both communications and active involvement.

At Harley-Davidson, top management is leading the learning revolution by example. CEO Richard Teerlink created a special twenty-person steering committee, reporting to the president, Jeff Bleustein. The committee is further broken down into three "circles": one focused on producing products (people from manufacturing, design, materials, and logistics), another on creating demand (people from dealerships, marketing, and riding clubs), and the third a group from corporate staff. As reported in Fortune,

> Members of the circles are top executives who meet at least once a month to conceive, analyze, and decide on ideas for improvement, new lines of business, and so on. An inner circle of eight, including Bleustein, also meets at least monthly and takes on the biggest ideas. . . . Harley's intersecting brainstorming circles are exactly the kind of accelerating device that companies need if they are to improve their ability to improve their abilities. Projects and task forces aren't enough, and all the tools and technology in the world won't

help if people aren't around to extract their lessons and convert them into better ways of getting better.[9]

At Tenneco, corporate leaders recognize that communications with their employees cannot be limited to crisis situations but must be part of an ongoing program to keep everyone informed of the company's plans, goals, and current status. Tenneco relies on the chain of command to get information to frontline employees. Writing in the *Harvard Business Review*, Thomas C. Hayes, special assistant to Tenneco's chairman and CEO, said:

> The focus of senior managers should be on getting facts into the hands of supervisors, whose job then is to lead and coach frontline workers on how changes will affect them. Tenneco uses variations on that approach in its four operating divisions, but not just when major changes have to be communicated. By then it's too late. Our goal is to get information to employees concurrent with important business developments.[10]

How can the company's top executives best handle their communications responsibilities? According to Hayes,

> There is no one best solution. Smartly produced videos, credible interviews with the news media, a CEO's letter to employees, computerized briefings, town hall meetings that last as long as the questions keep coming, and leadership conferences and retreats can be effective ways of getting supervisors to buy in to key messages.[11]

It is important that communications be a two-way street. True, communications from the CEO can help employees better understand the company's directions, plans, goals, and the like. But to foster a truly positive learning environment, the CEO must also demonstrate that there is much she or he can learn from employees. To do this means being involved in bi-directional dialogues with those employees. Karl Gretz and Steven

Drozdeck, in their book *Empowering Innovative People,* argue cogently for the involvement of senior executives:

> Get senior executives involved in the creative process. This is relatively easy to do and lends credibility to the work done by innovators. Periodically have a senior executive meet with groups of junior engineers, executives, marketing people, managers, etc., to discuss their vision of where the company is going, what it is doing right, and what it is doing wrong. This gives the senior manager an excellent opportunity to obtain effective insight into the thinking of his next generation of management.[12]

William Clover, director of the Amoco Management Learning Center, says that when top company executives first started coming to address groups of managers attending the company's renewal programs at the AMLC facility, they arrived in full dress uniform, asked for someone to handle their slides, and gave their hour-long presentation. But in those early sessions, the executives began to tune in to the audience, get involved in the discussions, listen to fresh ideas, and reveal some of their personal beliefs about the company and its renewal program. Clover says they "got hooked." In later sessions, they arrived in shirtsleeves, limited their presentations to a few pertinent slides, and just spent the time talking with the managers from the different business units, different levels within those business units, and the different countries in which Amoco does business. The executives' sessions became a highlight of the program, and much more learning took place (going in both directions) than was accomplished with the original formal presentations.

Leadership is not limited to the CEO and those occupying the highest levels of the company's organization chart. Leaders can and should come from all levels and functions. At one time, top officers were the only ones who were expected to have "an owner's perspective" on the business. According to Bossidy of AlliedSignal, "Yesterday, our employees had a worker's perspective on the business: keep your head down, do what you're told, don't ask questions. Today we're asking them to have an owner's perspective. We want employees to understand every aspect of the business, and not just their own function."[13]

Not all leaders are "born." To succeed in establishing a knowledge-enabled organization, leadership must be encouraged and nurtured at every level. According to Bossidy,

> Some people are, indeed, born leaders and you can spot them a mile away. The trouble is, there simply aren't enough of them to go around. So we need to find individuals with innate intelligence, an eagerness to learn, and a desire to work with others, and give them the tools and encouragement they need to become effective leaders, too. They may never run the company, but they can make enormous contributions to the success of your organization.[14]

Sometimes, the leader's greatest contribution to the learning environment can be to actively support the changes that are already happening—to recognize what is happening and then let it happen. Hughes Space and Communications' Arian Ward suggests:

> The key for leaders is to recognize the winds of change coming and to proactively prepare to integrate it into the business strategy and operations. Better yet, leaders themselves can use this revolutionary model to bring about changes they actively support, but they must be prepared to lead change in a new way. This model of leadership, which I follow myself, is best characterized by this quote from Disraeli: "There they go. I must follow them because I am their leader."[15]

This has been Jack Welch's approach with GE's famed WorkOut! sessions. By his very presence, he effectively empowers frontline employees to share their ideas and knowledge and makes a commitment to getting the best of those ideas implemented immediately by forcing these employees' managers to make on-the-spot decisions.

While strong, committed, visible leadership is a prerequisite in shaping a knowledge-enabled organization, it is not sufficient to cause the transformation. Other factors that must be examined and realigned to ensure that knowledge development and sharing take place in your company are changes in organizational structure, policies and procedures, and measurement and reward systems.

Organizational Structure

A financial and corporate services conglomerate that I visited is composed of several different businesses. Each started out as a stand-alone company before being acquired by the parent corporation. The CEO of the corporate parent is trying to get the various companies to share ideas and experiences, but he is having a difficult time because of the organizational structure. With its own culture and history, each subsidiary wants to continue to do business in its own way and is very wary of any ideas coming from other companies. For example, the United Kingdom branch of one business has spent two years building an outstanding customer service program that has won national and international awards for excellence. Attempts by the corporate parent to introduce the same program into its other businesses, and even into the United States arm of the same business, have met great resistance. "We're sure they've done a great job," say other executives, "but we're different. Our business is different, and the culture in the U.K. is very different from what we have here in the States."

There is some truth in these statements. The businesses are different. At the same time, customer service within the different businesses is more alike than different. The U.K. culture is different from the U.S. culture, but the similarities outweigh the differences. What causes these difficulties? The corporate organization continues to organize the businesses differently, treat each as a separate entity, and focus on the differences rather than the similarities. There is little or no contact among the different business units at any level below the CEO's staff meetings. Even on the corporate campus, the businesses are housed in separate buildings.

The separation of the business units is not only physical but also psychological. In essence, they are competing for the attention of the corporate staff, rather than working together to create a better future for the overall corporation. There is little movement of personnel between business units. Each continues to have its own ways of organizing, hiring and training, and doing business.

These problems are not limited to the conglomerate type of corporation. They exist in many companies that are in a single business. To cite two examples, smokestack and silo types of organizations do not allow for cross-fertilization of ideas and knowledge. Whether the separation of business units, functions, and departments is physical or organizational, the result is the same: People cannot share knowledge if they are effectively barred from talking and working with one another. In this way, small companies have a real advantage over larger companies because organizational boundaries have not had time to develop. Says Arthur Andersen's Robert J. Hiebeler, "In small companies where people routinely observe others and work in close physical proximity, it is easier to transmit tacit knowledge than in large companies where people are increasingly not located with either their own work teams or teams that have parallel or similar experiences." Hiebeler also identifies the factor he considers most critical to building a knowledge-enabled organization: "An organization must be willing to reengineer its organizational structures and take a long-term view of the potential benefits of developing a knowledge leveraging strategy."[16]

Merck CEO Gilmartin tore down functional and geographic boundaries by creating "worldwide business strategy teams" focusing on specific diseases. "The teams bring together executives from areas as diverse as finance, manufacturing, and marketing to assess everything from drugs' production costs to market potential." Gilmartin's philosophy is, "Where you want the contest is not among people but among ideas."[17]

At the extreme of organizational change is Danish hearing aid maker Oticon. To rebound from a near corporate disaster, President Lars Kolind instituted what he calls the "spaghetti revolution": tearing down the old organizational structure and not replacing it with any identifiable structure at all. An *Industry Week* report reveals the audacity of the solution:

> This revolution, as described by Kolind, involved stripping away almost every vestige of the past: no more hierarchy, no corner offices, no memos, no set hours. The past was thrown off, and in its place came, to use Kolind's word, "chaos." This was necessary, he said, because "it takes chaos to produce a breakthrough." What remained was a "spaghetti organization"— defined by Kolind as "a knowledge-based company that looks like and works like the brain. And a brain is a disorganized, chaotic collection of capabilities with a very spaghetti-like communications structure."[18]

Has chaos worked for Oticon? Definitely. Worldwide market share has risen from 7 percent in 1988 to 15 percent today. Sales are up 57 percent in the past three years. Do I recommend this "form of organization" for all companies? Not unless you study Kolind's efforts and believe that what worked for Oticon will work for you.

This book does not offer a new organizational form; there are many suggested in other books and successfully practiced. Few companies will ever reach the goal that Jack Welch has set for GE: to become a "boundaryless organization." But whatever form your company's organization takes, it must have open boundaries at every level, across which information flows easily; boundaries easily crossed by employees seeking to share their knowledge and skills with others and in turn learn from them. Without these permeable boundaries, the knowledge-enabled organization cannot exist.

Policies and Procedures

If every employee's work is so bound by company policies and procedures that there is no room for change, opportunity for improvement, or access to other parts of the organization, then there can be no new knowledge created. Policies and procedures that were instituted long ago to help define jobs, make employees' work easier to do, and ensure standards of excellence in the company's products and services can stifle creativity, knowledge sharing, and progress today. Many of yesterday's greatest corporate successes instituted thousands of policies and procedures to promote orderly growth. Today, these policy and procedures manuals are lead weights, dragging progress to the murky depths.

Policies and procedures tend to make any organization reactionary because they are typically based on past experience. As Gretz and Drozdeck state in *Empowering Innovative People*:

> Because of the reactionary nature of any system, it is natural for a manager to spend more time trying to maintain what he has and understands than to take risks with something new. Hence, when employees or junior managers offer innovations to procedures, policies, or products, they are often perceived as a threat rather than as a resource.[19]

There is no set of recommended universal policies and procedures to enable or facilitate building a knowledge-enabled organization. The caveat here is that as your company tries to build a positive learning environment and become a knowledge-enabled organization, you should examine your policies and procedures, both explicit and tacit, to ensure that they are not working at cross-purposes with your goals.

Measurements and Rewards

You can never get employees to adopt new behaviors if you continue to measure and reward them on the basis of the old behaviors. This simple truth has defeated many a company's renewal or transformation program.

If we want employees to build their own capabilities to get the job done, and if we want to encourage employees to share their knowledge with others, we need to structure our measurement and reward systems to reflect these priorities.

At Ernst & Young, getting people to contribute to the knowledge databases wasn't easy. U.S. Chief Knowledge Officer John Peetz compared the task to "dental extraction." The solution was to use measurements and rewards to encourage use: "Now, at the end of the year, one-fourth of a person's annual performance review is based on his or her contribution to the knowledge process. . . . Junior associates are graded on the sheer quantity of their submissions, with extra points if their contribution is selected for inclusion in [the knowledge base]."[20]

At Buckman Laboratories, employees are measured on how much knowledge they create and how much they share with others through the knowledge network. After the first year of the network's operation, the 150 most active users of the network were gathered at a resort in Arizona to discuss the network's future. Besides the trip, they were rewarded with new personal computers, leather computer cases, and other perquisites.

Building a Technical Infrastructure to Support the Knowledge-Enabled Organization

Knowledge sharing is about communications. Unless yours is a small organization where employees are located in relatively compact premises, the company needs to provide technologies and tools to promote communications. Businesses of all sizes and types are inundated with pitches for the latest and greatest technologies: mainframe-based data warehouses; local area networks of personal computers; telephone-, computer-, and video-conferencing; corporate networks; the Internet and intranets; cellular phones; beepers; and e-mail.

No one solution can work for every company. But it is equally true that people cannot communicate or share their knowledge without some type of technology infrastructure that makes it both possible and easy. As previously noted, companies should work with their own information systems and telecommunications groups or providers to explore which options best fit their situations. But make no mistake: Information and communications technology is a key contributor to the knowledge-enabled organization. Says Edward E. Lawler III, director of the Center for Effective Organizations at the University of Southern California School of Business, "Information technology and what it can do to give people skills and the ability to behave very differently in the workplace will be the strongest driving force for change in how we think about organizations and how we manage people."[21]

A strong technical infrastructure can support the knowledge-enabled organization, but is not sufficient to make it happen.

Even if a company aligns its policies and procedures, changes its measurement and reward systems, demonstrates commitment on the part of top leadership to becoming a knowledge-enabled organization, and installs the best information systems and telecommunications equipment, there is always a lot of inertial resistance to change. My own experience is that once people start sharing knowledge and seeing the benefits to themselves and others, they hunger for more opportunities to do so. But it takes considerable effort to get these programs started.

Jump-Starting the Knowledge-Enabled Organization

There are many ways to boost your efforts. The following vignettes suggest what has worked for some companies; they are offered as worthwhile ideas that you can adapt to your own company's situation, capabilities, and culture.

* At Buckman Laboratories, contests were held to encourage use of the company's new knowledge network. Prizes were awarded to those who guessed, for example, the date and time that the five-hundredth and one-thousandth messages would be posted to the discussion forums. Along with such incentives, Buckman also "forced" some usage. For example, a person calling a headquarters group with a question was told that they would take the question over the phone this one time, but that the question and answer would be posted on the knowledge network. Over time, some headquarters groups then moved to declining to answer questions that were not posted in the discussion forums.

＊ Gretz and Drozdeck report that "The director of R&D at one medical chemical company requires his scientists to work regularly with their customers. Not only does this give them a better idea of what the customer needs, it also lets them bask in the customer's appreciation when they deliver a product they created at the customer's request."[22] This helps the scientists learn more about customer needs and how customers use the products they develop.

＊ At many scientific conferences, poster sessions allow scientists to share their ideas, methods, and findings with colleagues from other institutions.

＊ At a major toy manufacturer, Gretz and Drezdock relate, "the R&D department . . . regularly holds both informal and formal 'show and tell' sessions. Like a requirement for publication, these sessions provide each designer with regular feedback and praise from both peers and superiors, and also remind them of their accountability for their goals."[23]

＊ When holding regular staff meetings with the managers who work for her, one CEO starts by asking each manager what that group has learned since the last meeting.

＊ One service manager requires any employee making a major diagnostic error to write up the case and put it in the knowledge base so that others can learn from it. The manager then rewards the employee for adding to the company's knowledge. (This rewarding is very important: When we make mistakes, we tend to forget about them. By publicizing them, we can help others avoid the negative "value" of making the same mistakes in the future, and attaching incentives acknowledges the positive value of learning through errors.)

＊ Knowledge-enabled companies use employee suggestion systems as primary sources of ideas. *Industry Week* reports that

"Wainwright Industries Inc., in St. Peters, Missouri, implemented an average of sixty suggestions per associate in 1995—200 times the U.S. average of 0.3 suggestions per employee. At Wainwright, the cumulative impact of many small improvements has produced such results as a 70.3 percent reduction in scrap and rework and a 99 percent reduction in manufacturing cycle time on stamped housings."[24]

✳ An article in the *Harvard Business Review* says that at Arthur Andersen, "To stimulate a cultural shift toward wider use of ANet [the Andersen Worldwide knowledge network], senior partners deliberately posed questions on employees' e-mail files each morning 'to be answered by ten.' Until those cultural changes were in place, ANet was less than successful despite its technical elegance."[25]

In the early 1980s, I was manager of networks education and training (part of the networks and communications world) at Digital Equipment Corporation. At that time, networks were about to be revolutionized by the introduction of local area networks. Digital was getting ready to lead the revolution from an engineering standpoint, but its field-based personnel in both sales and service were not ready to sell, install, and service the products. With the cooperation of the many corporate groups that were working on this new generation of communications technology, we created a learning environment that is yet to be surpassed at Digital or anywhere else. The cornerstone of these efforts was a program I created that became known as Network University.

Digital's Network University

A key to Digital's increasing network-related sales from $400 million to more than $1 billion in less than four years was the establishment of district network teams, or DNTs, composed of key sales, field service, and software services personnel. Working as a team, they would provide a high-level focus on network sales in each of the company's thirty-six U.S. sales districts.

When these teams were first assembled, each district selected its own model; some teams included one person from each discipline, others had one salesperson and multiple representatives from field service and software, and still others had multiple representatives from each discipline. At an early organizational meeting, team members identified their number-one concern: getting sufficient training and easy access to the technical information they needed to be effective in their new roles.

To meet these needs, the corporate networks and communications organization developed several critical strategies:

✳ Members of the DNTs were given direct access to technical back-up people at the corporate level.

✳ Online discussion forums were created to foster discussion of network-related issues and to allow field-based and corporate personnel to ask questions and learn from each other. Digital had, at that time, the largest private data network in the world, and every person in networking had a direct connection. The company also had some internally developed tools for holding these discussions (known as "notes files"). While they were relatively unsophisticated and not nearly as user friendly as today's products, they got the job done.

✳ Corporate groups responsible for marketing communications, field programs, and technical support provided a steady flow of information and tools to field personnel to help them plan and execute sales strategies. These included sales kits, physical models to represent how buildings could be wired for local area networks, product information sheets, demonstration software, etc.

✳ I created semiannual, week-long Network University learning events for field personnel. Some training took place during these sessions, but I call them learning events because many modes of learning took place during each week.

The components of the learning environment created for and by Network University should be understood in terms of:

✳ How content was determined
✳ How learning resources were selected

* How participants learned
* How the events were organized
* How learning was evaluated

Determining the Content of Network University

The content of each Network University program was first determined by asking the participants (the DNTs) what they needed to learn. While they focused primarily on technical information, we also received requests to include training on topics such as making the business case for networking and how to prepare a proposal for business managers (rather than for the technical managers to whom Digital traditionally sold).

At the same time, we recognized that there were topical areas that the DNT members "didn't know they didn't know," namely, new products and services about to be introduced by the company. We determined these topics by asking product managers and marketing managers what was in the development pipeline. Other topics for the program came from such sources as:

* Corporate back-up support groups, asked what areas seemed to consume most of their time (that is, which topical areas seemed to be generating the most questions, discussions, or confusion among the field personnel the groups supported)
* Corporate competitive analysis groups, for topics on major current and future competitors and trends in the networks field
* Strategic planning groups, to do sessions on future trends

Selecting Learning Resources

Because networking technology was evolving so rapidly in the 1980s, preparing professional trainers to run the Network University sessions was impossible. In actuality, the time from determining a program's content to the delivery of that content was less than three months, with approximately 80 percent of the content being new for each program. Our strategy was to use subject-matter experts (SMEs) for all sessions, to find the most knowledgeable resource person for each topic area. These included engineers, marketing personnel, strategic planners, competitive analysts, internal telecommunications managers . . . anyone and everyone in Digital's networks world was eligible. In several cases, we asked members of the DNTs to do sessions themselves, to share their knowledge and experience with others. Where we couldn't find an internal resource, we went outside, using consultants, university professors, professional industry watchers, personnel from cooperating vendors, etc.

Because virtually none of these learning resource people had training experience, we provided them with some guidelines for preparing their presentations. We also matched presenters with members of the target audience so that they could test their ideas for sessions to be sure that what they were planning to do would meet the audience's needs. Not every presenter made use of these resources. In fact, when a session failed dramatically (as in having no audience left at the end of a session), it was almost always the case that the presenter had not used the field resource to test the session beforehand. Two basic instructions to all presenters were to leave time for questions and to be both totally open to questions and totally frank in giving answers.

At one session, a product manager was to talk about how her product—introduced four months before the session—could be used to leverage network sales. Although she agreed to create a session on this topic, she didn't do it. Instead, she took the product introduction presentation off the shelf and started to give it in her session. After five minutes, someone interrupted: "Why did I travel three thousand miles to hear you give a presentation that I have given several dozen times myself?" The questioner then got a standing ovation from the rest of the audience. (It was a tough crowd.)

The product manager recovered well. She apologized for not preparing the presentation she had promised, stopped the one she was giving, and took questions for the rest of the session. That discussion was probably more valuable to the participants than any presentation she could have created beforehand.

It should be noted that many of the presenters initially balked at doing these sessions. ("You want me—an engineer—to talk to salespeople? What value is there in that? It will be a total waste of my time!") The first engineering participants, although reluctant, got a great surprise: They actually learned a lot from the field personnel. After they got back to their offices and told their colleagues about their experiences, we had many engineering volunteers for the next program.

This is a very important point. The learning resource people who participated in Network University were not just there to share their knowledge with the field-based participants; they were there to learn from them as well. The free exchange of knowledge, ideas, and experiences was what made Network University such a unique and effective learning experience for all participants.

How Participants Learned

Each Network University program, running from Sunday evening to early Friday afternoon, overflowed with information in several formats:

* Information everyone needed—say, an upcoming new product—was handled in a general session with everyone attending.
* Information sessions on specific products, services, and technologies took from one to two hours.
* In demonstration sessions, participants could see the equipment and applications firsthand and actually try them out.
* Training sessions on focused topics, for example, configuring local area networks, were given from half a day to two full days.

✳ Guest speakers, typically external experts on a given topic, talked at lunch or dinner sessions.

As good as these formal sessions generally were, more learning took place outside those sessions than inside. From early morning until late at night, members of the DNTs met, discussed their experiences, related "war stories," and learned what tactics and solutions had worked or not worked for others. Recognizing what was happening and how valuable these informal sessions were to the participants, we facilitated them. At some meals, we designated "topic tables": "For those interested, please look for the Table A at lunch." On some afternoons, we held "birds-of-a-feather" sessions, where all people interested in Topic B could "flock together" in a given room. In organizing the topic tables and birds-of-a-feather sessions, we recruited product managers, engineers, and other expert resources to attend. We also rescheduled luncheon and dinner speakers away from some meals to allow more time for informal discussions.

Organizing Network University Events

A typical Network University program had forty to seventy separate sessions, with as many as five taking place simultaneously. How did we assign participants to the sessions? We didn't. Participants self-selected the sessions they would attend based on schedules, session descriptions, and their own learning needs. Some regional and district teams planned ahead of time to have at least one person attend every session given. To compensate for those times when more than one concurrent session was of interest to an individual participant, we gave everyone the handouts from all sessions.

As the audience for the Network University programs continued to expand, with many new network-related jobs opening up in the field organization, we put together a two-day "boot camp" to quickly indoctrinate these new participants before they attended the Network University program.

It should be noted that we did not allow every suggested topic onto the Network University agenda. Once the program was well known, many corporate groups requested time on the agenda to spread their own messages. If the topic was central to the network's theme, we tried to accommodate them. When it was clearly not related, we rejected them. For a topic in a gray area, we offered to include materials in the packages we prepared for the participants, whether a printed handout or a videotape or audiocassette.

Evaluating Network University Sessions

Each session in Network University was evaluated on three criteria:

1. The relevance of the session to the participant's work
2. The added value the session brought to the participant
3. The quality of the session

While these measures were useful, we found that participants voted with their feet. If a session was poor, they literally walked out—generally, there were other sessions going on concurrently, and if one wasn't good, perhaps another would be better. Leaving a session also freed more time for those important informal interactions with other participants.

Because we often had seventy to one hundred different presenters at a given Network University program, it was impossible to screen them and their material beforehand. At every program, there were a few bad sessions. But a presenter never presented two bad sessions in a row. Because our audience was so vocal, presenters knew immediately when they had missed the mark. In some cases, they came up with an immediate recovery plan, as did the product manager discussed earlier. Or the presenters would apologize to the audience and promise to do better next time (and generally did so). In a few cases, the presenters didn't care that they missed the mark; they weren't invited back.

Lessons From Network University

Digital's Network University and the other learning activities furthering the work of the district network teams could not have succeeded without a number of changes to support the development of a positive learning environment:

✳ Leadership from the top of the networks organization tore down long-standing barriers to cooperation among corporate groups, such as marketing, engineering, field support, and manufacturing. Leaders of all of these corporate groups not only supported the programs with their personnel but they personally participated in the programs. Without the cooperation of all of these groups and their working toward the single goal of increasing network-related sales, none of these efforts could have succeeded. In the past, engineering, for example, might have scoffed at the idea of training salespeople as not their job.

✳ At the district as well as corporate levels, there were strong barriers to cooperation among sales, software services, and field service. We were never totally successful in tearing down these barriers, but we took advantage of the looseness of the Digital organization that allowed local representatives from these groups to essentially make their own decisions on what programs to support (sometimes even when their superiors at the corporate level openly fought the programs).

✳ Standard company policies and procedures for field support were examined, and where they could not support the goals of the network's sales effort, they were changed—or ignored.

✳ Corporate leadership worked with local management to create new measurement-and-reward systems for the DNTs. The old system of measurements and rewards did not foster cooperation among the various functions represented on the teams and would have contravened the goals of these programs. Where necessary, corporate groups instituted their own recognition-and-reward programs for the field resources.

✳ Communications within the network world, both at the Network University events and between sessions, were totally open. No question was barred, and every participant was instructed to give totally open and honest answers. The only exceptions to this rule were in cases where giving an honest answer might adversely affect some ongoing negotiation or legal action. In these cases, participants were told that the answer could not be provided and why not, and that they would be given the answer as soon as it was possible to do so.

Network University created an unsurpassed learning environment for technical information.[26] Many of the participants were recent hires from other high-technology companies, and they were amazed by its power and energy.

Is it possible to create this type of dynamic learning environment in your company? Yes, definitely. However, the learning environment depends not just on training programs but on the wide array of issues addressed in this chapter.

Notes

1. Nathan Rosenberg, "Uncertainty and Technological Change," paper prepared for the Federal Bank of Boston's Conference on Technology and Growth, June 5–7, 1996, p. 12.
2. Bennett Harrison, "The Importance of Being Complementary," *Technology Review*, October 1996, p. 65.
3. Lawrence A. Bossidy, "Reality-Based Leadership," in a speech to the Economic Club of Washington, D.C., June 19, 1996.
4. Michael A. Cusumano, and Richard W. Selby, *Microsoft Secrets: How the World's Most Powerful Software Company Creates Technology* (New York: The Free Press, 1995), pp. 327–328). Copyright 1995 by Michael A. Cusumano and Richard W. Selby. Reprinted with permission of The Free Press, a Division of Simon & Schuster.
5. Ibid., p. 105.
6. Polly Labarre, "How Skandia Generates Its Future Faster," *Fast Company*, December–January 1997, p. 58.
7. "Mr. Nice Guy with a Mission," *Business Week*, November 25, 1996, p. 132, 136.
8. "Senior Execs Champion Organizational Learning," *Knowledge Inc.*, June 1996, p. 5.
9. Thomas Stewart, "Tools that Make the Business Better and Better," *Fortune*, CompuServe Online Edition, December 23, 1996. © 1996 Time Inc. All rights reserved.
10. "Letter to the Editor," *Harvard Business Review*, September–October 1996, p. 190.
11. Ibid.
12. Karl F. Gretz, and Steven R. Drozdeck, *Empowering Innovative People*

(Burr Ridge, Ill.: Irwin Professional Publishing, 1994; excerpt published in the CompuServe *Industry Week* forum).

13. "Reality-Based Leadership," address by Lawrence A. Bossidy, chairman and CEO, AlliedSignal, to the Economic Club of Washington, D.C., June 19, 1996.
14. Ibid.
15. Arian Ward, "Lessons Learned on the Knowledge Highways and Byways," *Strategy & Leadership*, March–April 1996, pp. 16–20.
16. Robert J. Hiebeler, "Benchmarking Knowledge Management," *Strategy & Leadership*, March–April 1996, pp. 22–28.
17. "Mr. Nice Guy with a Mission," p. 136.
18. Edward Walsh, "An All-Star Lineup," *Industry Week*, CompuServe Online Edition, December 2, 1996.
19. Gretz and Drozdeck, op. cit.
20. David Bank, "Know-It-Alls," *Wall Street Journal*, November 18, 1996, p. R28.
21. Michael A. Verespej, "A Workforce Revolution?" *Industry Week*, August 21, 1995 (from the CompuServe *Industry Week* forum).
22. Gretz and Drozdeck, op. cit.
23. Ibid.
24. "America's Best Plants—The Winners," *Industry Week*, CompuServe Online Edition, October 7, 1996.
25. James Brian Quinn, Philip Anderson, and Sydney Finkelstein, "Managing Professional Intellect," *Harvard Business Review*, March–April 1996, p. 76.
26. On a management level, one program that is probably its match is Amoco's Management Learning Center, described in my book *Transformational Learning: Renewing Your Company Through Knowledge and Skills* (New York: John Wiley & Sons, 1996).

8

Throw Out the Training Catalog, Not the Training Group

The art of teaching is the art of assisting discovery.

Mark Van Doren

If, as I have argued, the traditional approach to training and development cannot meet the learning needs of today's company, what should you do with your well-established training groups? Should you, as many companies have done, include them on the list for the next corporate downsizing? Or should you, as many other companies continue to do, simply ignore them, letting them continue business as usual with the hope that they add some value to the company? Neither option is acceptable.

We try to ensure that every function is closely aligned with the company's strategic business directions. We try to make every group within the company's boundaries aware of its role in major business processes and require them to work cross-functionally to improve business results. We must expect the same of the training and development group. Somehow, it has managed to stay out of the loop, perhaps helping other groups' transformations but never transforming itself. In the knowledge-enabled organization, the training and development group is not exempt from these changes; it is an active force in transforming itself and facilitating the company's transformation.

I propose that we change the name of this group to reflect its new role in the knowledge-enabled organization. Rather than "training and development" or "human resource development," I recommend that it be named "employee and organizational learning." I also recommend that the first step the new group takes to demonstrate its transformation should be to throw out the traditional training catalog.

Throw Out the Training Catalog

At the AlliedSignal Aerospace facilities in Phoenix, Arizona, the training catalog used to be published quarterly. It has not been published for several years. Instead, a manager or employee wanting to take a formerly offered course must call the human resources department. A consultant then determines why the caller wants to take the particular course. If, from this interview, the course seems to solve the problem, then it can be scheduled. More often, the consultant discovers that there isn't really a training problem or that other learning activities can be suggested that more directly address the employee's needs.

When a training catalog is published, employees tend to look at the array of courses as their primary means for learning: "These are the courses that the company has created for me and my fellow employees, so there must be some value in them." But only a small fraction of employees' learning needs are covered by courses in the catalog, and little of the training content of those courses ever gets transformed into knowledge through application to the employees' work.

Training catalogs reflect the past and limit the potential for real learning.

Working in a corporate training department, I sometimes met with students at the end of a course. I often asked, "Why did you take this course?" The variety of answers I received clearly demonstrates the problem with traditional training programs:

* "My development plan calls for me to take a course this year, and this looks interesting."
* "It's my turn to take a training course."
* "My boss was so pleased with my work on my last project, she told me I could take a course this month; this is the most relevant one on the schedule."
* "I thought the content of the course might help me with my next project."
* "My group is changing computer systems, and I thought it would be wise to learn something about the new system."
* "My boss and I had a major blow-up, and he told me to go take a course for a week so that we would both have time to cool down."
* "My manager took this course last year and liked it so much he's having everyone in the group take it."
* " We're in a lull in our business cycle, so it looks like a good time to take a course."

Are these good reasons to take a course, no matter what its content? Based on these answers, how much learning do you think took place in the courses? How many of these students are going to apply the course content to their jobs? Given their reasons for taking a course, these students may have fulfilled personal needs, or a need of their manager's, or fulfilled a requirement in their development plans. But little or no learning takes place, and there is virtually no transfer of learning back to the job.

When a traditional training group publishes a training catalog and schedule, it looks to the past, not to the future. Why? Training catalogs are collections of courses that have been developed over the years, based on how the company worked at the time each course was developed. Once a course enters the catalog, it rarely leaves, thereby perpetuating past practice.

Traditional training groups usually don't have any mechanism to monitor if what they are teaching corresponds to current business practice. If a student or manager tells a trainer, "That's not the way we do things any longer—we changed our methods," the trainer typically responds, "We'll look into that the next time we revise the course." However long that "regular review cycle" takes—if it exists at all—the training group continues teaching out-of-date methods or passing along old information until a review is done, the materials are revised, the trainers are retrained, etc. It can take years to change a course once it appears in the training catalog.

Using standardized training programs also creates another learning problem. In a given class, you have a range of student knowledge and abilities. If you mark those levels on a scale of 0 to 100, the typical instructional program teaches at the level of 15–20. This means that those people who are in the 21–100 range learn little that is new to them. Trainers pick this target so that those most in need of new knowledge and skills are served; if they trained at the 80 level, they would leave most of the class behind.

Publishing a training catalog also limits employees' thinking about how they can learn. The training catalog makes the employee dependent on the training group in three ways:

1. Some employees believe that if it isn't in the training catalog, it can't be important: "I'm supposed to learn about X for my job. But if the company doesn't think X is important enough to offer a course on it, maybe I don't really need to learn about X."
2. Some employees feel that their only learning options are those in the catalog: "I need to learn about X. But that course isn't going to be offered until next year. I'll just keep doing things the old way until the course is available. What choice do I have?"
3. Some employees feel that the training group knows more about what they need to learn than they and their managers know: "I need to learn about X. The only thing in the training catalog that includes X is the course that covers T through Z. Well, maybe I'll learn something else of value if I take the course."

What happens to employees when you throw out the training catalog? They begin to take responsibility for locating their own learning resources. Working with their managers through the medium of their individual learning contracts, employees identify their own learning needs and find the best available learning resources wherever they reside, inside or outside the company. Employees can still approach the company's training group to ask if the group could offer a course to help them learn. But if they find that a course offered by the training group doesn't meet their needs, they can negotiate for its revision—or they can even bypass the training group in favor of other, more appropriate learning resources.

What happens to the training group when you throw out the training catalog? Trainers and instructional designers suddenly find a different purpose in life. The training catalog defined their professional existence for them: "We create courses and we train employees." Now the people in the training group have to redefine themselves. This new definition starts with the name change to EOL, employee and organizational learning.

The Employee and Organizational Learning Group

Traditional training groups must change their focus to enabling and facilitating individual and organizational learning.

The employee and organizational learning group focuses on learning rather than training. *Learning* focuses on the employee—the person doing the learning—whereas *training* focuses on the trainer. In the knowledge-enabled organization, only the employee and her manager can determine what is to be learned to improve individual and organizational performance. With this change in focus come new requirements for members of the EOL group:

* Working with employees and managers, teaching them how to identify learning needs and translate them into learning requirements and contracts
* Working with the company's information services de-

partment to design the knowledge network and then take responsibility for building and maintaining its content

* Researching and publishing "learning guides" rather than training catalogs
* Coaching employees at all levels on how to identify and utilize internal and external learning resources
* Teaching all employees how to best share their knowledge with others

Former trainers might now go on developing courses and doing some training as the need arises—so long as the training content, new or old, is closely aligned with a business goal.

Teaching Employees to Identify Learning Needs

Making each employee responsible for identifying his own learning needs is a major shift for most companies. To be successful with this new style, both employees and their managers need to learn how to translate job requirements into learning needs. The EOL group can develop procedures for doing this; it can first instruct, and then coach, employees and managers on how to follow those procedures. (As employees, managers, and the EOL group members themselves gain experience in doing this, a formal competency system may or may not evolve, depending on the stability and commonality among identified learning needs.)

Another area where the EOL group can take a lead role is in developing baseline measurements, that is, in helping assess employees' current knowledge and skill levels. Recall that before new learning needs can be identified, you need to assess both employees' goals and their current levels of knowledge and skill related to those goals. In this way, learning activities can be tailored to exact learning needs and learning levels. An employee at the 20 level undertakes 20-level learning activities while one at the 90 level seeks learning activities at that high level.

EOL staff can also act as counselors to employees at all levels, helping them to identify their learning needs and to locate appropriate learning resources and learning methods, both within and without the company. The Canadian Imperial Bank of Commerce has set up a series of career centers, whose employees act in this counseling capacity along with carrying out other duties.

Building and Maintaining the Knowledge Network

Most knowledge networks are technology-based. Indeed, at Buckman Laboratories, the information services group has been renamed the "knowledge transfer department." Although the selection of hardware, software, and communications services for the knowledge network falls to technical experts, the EOL group should work with those experts in designing the knowledge databases and networks. The group should take the lead in building and maintaining the content of the databases and discussion forums, and in teaching employees at all levels how to utilize these new tools (as described in Chapter 6). EOL activities related to the knowledge networks may include:

 * Defining content of the knowledge databases, including selecting and assigning keywords to entries for better organization and easier searching of the databases. Keywords are an essential element of the knowledge network. Discipline and consistency in usage ensure that employees seeking information from the databases can find what they want.

 * Acting as section leaders, where EOL staff have the appropriate subject matter expertise (see Chapter 6).

 * Monitoring activity in the databases and discussion forums to identify learning needs that may require new learning resources, for example, new sections in databases or new learning tools, courses, etc. If the same question keeps arising in the discussion forums, it means that employees have not been able to find the answer in the databases, documentation, or training. This points to a need for a new training program, new or better documentation, or a new entry in the knowledge database.

 * Organizing new learning groups or activities. If EOL staff find a number of employees seeking learning resources on a given topic, they can (1) organize a learning group whose members can help each other learn, (2) offer to develop a new

learning program, or (3) help find an internal or external learning resource for the learners.

＊ Constantly monitoring the external environment to identify—and then include in the learning resources database— information on external courses, conferences, symposia, seminars, books, articles, research reports, etc.

Researching and Publishing Learning Guides

Learning guides (such as those developed by the Canadian Imperial Bank of Commerce and PPG Industries) help employees fulfill their learning contracts by pointing them to a variety of resources they can use to meet their learning requirements. In Chapter 4, we clarified that these guides are more than just training catalogs. They include a variety of learning methods and resources for any given topic: internal and external courses, audiovisual and computer-based instructional resources, books, articles, and so on.

Constant updating of these guides helps employees easily identify the best available knowledge resources. Where these resources are people rather than materials or courses, the learning guides should also suggest *how* employees can learn from other employees: through dialogues in the discussion forums on the knowledge network, apprenticeships, job rotation, mentoring relationships, and still other means.

Coaching Employees to Identify and Utilize Learning Resources

EOL staff, therefore, should also coach employees at all levels on how to identify and utilize internal and external learning resources. As with any change in long-standing practice, switching from dependency on a training catalog to becoming our own learning guide requires practice, coaching, and reinforcement. This applies not only to frontline employees but also to managers. (How often have we told managers that they must start coaching their employees in trying out new skills, yet we offer the managers themselves no coaching as they try out *their* newly acquired coaching skills?) Essentially, the EOL staff needs to teach employees and managers at all levels how to take responsibility for their own learning activities.

Developing Courseware and Offering Formal Courses

The EOL staff may also retain some of the group's former responsibility for developing and teaching formal courses, but only when there is a demonstrated business need for the course. By monitoring employees' learning contracts, EOL staff can identify those learning topics for which there may be sufficient demand for a course or some other learning tool. This monitoring activity is much easier if learning contracts are put into a database so they can be analyzed to examine common learning needs among employees, regardless of level, function, or location.

Teaching Knowledge Resource People How to Share Their Knowledge

In the knowledge-enabled organization, all employees are not only learners but also knowledge resources that can be called upon by other employees to share their knowledge. Given that sharing one's knowledge is not the current norm in most corporations, employees have to learn on their own how best to share their knowledge with others. Methods range from answering questions posted in the knowledge network's discussion forums to mentoring and coaching, to writing training materials and teaching classes, to creating a knowledge document and placing it in the knowledge database. For most employees, these are brand new skills. The job of teaching employees how to share their knowledge should fall to the EOL group.

It is important to note that since the EOL group no longer has sole responsibility for the company's training/learning activities, you have to reorient the members of that group as well as teach every employee to take responsibility for her own learning and to become a knowledge resource for other employees.

Employee Responsibilities in the Knowledge-Enabled Organization

In a knowledge-enabled organization, all employees are responsible for their own learning; they also contribute their own knowledge to help meet the learning needs of other employees. This is very different from traditional corporate cultures, where employees are told "You don't get paid to think—managers think—you do your work" or "Get your own work done—don't worry about anything but your own work."

In addition to developing and fulfilling the terms of his own learning contract, each employee should also regularly use—and, a somewhat different thing, *participate* in—the knowledge network. Here are guidelines for employee participation in the knowledge network:

* Monitor forums daily, or at least every few days. If you can answer a question, or clarify a question or answer, do so. But don't idly speculate.
* Be familiar with documentation, training materials, library files, databases, etc., so that you know how to use them to find answers to your own questions. In this way, you won't ask questions that have already been answered elsewhere.
* If you have a question, ask it in the appropriate discussion forum, even if you have already found the answer. This is because if you have a question, others probably have the same one.
* If you see an incorrect answer being given, say so and tell why it is wrong, even if you don't have the correct answer yourself. In this way, you can help others avoid mistakes you have made—even if you haven't yet discovered how to avoid the mistake yourself.
* If you don't know an answer but know someone who probably does, take responsibility for asking that person to follow up and answer the question.
* If you participate in a discussion (with coworkers, customers, suppliers, conference attendees, or otherwise)

that yields new knowledge, write it up and post it in the forum.

✴ If you read a book or article, hear a presentation at a conference, or run across other relevant information, post it in the forum so that others can also learn from it.

✴ If you have an idea for a new product or service, a new market for an existing product or service, an improvement in how the company does its work, etc., post it for discussion.

Managers also have responsibility for fostering their employees' participation (as well as their own) in the knowledge network. They should:

✴ Participate in the discussion forums equally with all other employees.

✴ Encourage employees to actively participate in the forums.

✴ Measure and reward employees both for using the forums as a learning tool and for contributing their own knowledge to the forums.

✴ Encourage an employee demonstrating new knowledge (a new application for an existing product; a new, more efficient way of doing work) to share that knowledge in the appropriate forum.

Organizing the Employee and Organizational Learning Group

Traditional training groups usually reside within the human resources department—one reason why trainers have generally been outside the mainstream of the company's business. The employee and organizational learning group cannot be so hidden from the business. I recommend a "hub and spokes" model of organization for the EOL group.

At the hub is a group of people with traditional expertise in learning theory, instructional design, and training skills. This hub acts as a corporate resource. It should be responsible for building and maintaining the knowledge network, monitoring trends in learning needs as identified from employee learning contracts, and building and maintaining the learning guides.

The spokes of the wheel reach out into the various business units and staff functions of the corporation and act as learning consultants to those groups. Depending on the size of the overall group, EOL staff may serve a dual function: being part of the hub with specific learning-related skills, and at the same time acting as a consultant to one or more business groups. As a consultant, the EOL staffer coaches employees and managers on learning and knowledge-sharing skills, keeps track of trends in the business and the resulting learning needs, and is the liaison between the business units and the core EOL group. As effective business partners, these consultants must learn consulting skills and develop a basic understanding of the business. They diagnose how business challenges can be translated into learning needs or other types of change requirements, whether those are changes in job design, organizational change, or other types of organizational development; changes in policies and procedures; measurement and reward systems; and so forth. This change in roles from what is traditionally associated with the training function requires a lot of learning *on the part of EOL staff*—a subject that is often overlooked.

The Learning Needs of the EOL Staff

Training groups don't pay enough attention to the learning needs of their own members. In changing from the traditional training model to the employee and organizational learning model, we have to ask former instructional designers and trainers to acquire a lot of new knowledge and learn many new skills:

* The company's business and its basic business vocabulary
* Consultation skills
* Diagnostic skills related to employee learning, organizational development, and other aspects of the business
* Collaboration with the information services group on

using and maintaining the various components of the
knowledge network
* Perhaps most difficult of all, how to help people lacking
the trainer's background (in instructional design and
learning theory) learn to share their knowledge through
a wide variety of methods—most of which have not been
in the traditional trainer's repertoire

Establishing a knowledge-enabled organization is a shock
to every employee in the company. It requires them to change
their basic ways of working and to take personal responsibility
for their own learning and job performance. But change is perhaps hardest of all for members of the traditional training group.
We are asking these people to abandon the world they have
spent years building and in effect tear it down and replace it
with a world they may view, from their own training and experience, as inferior. Not every training group can make this transi-
tion.

Comparing the Traditional Training Group and the EOL Group

Table 8.1 compares the traditional training group with the employee and organizational learning group on eight criteria.
    Certain of the criteria in Table 8.1 deserve elaboration to
better understand how the EOL group differs from traditional
training groups:

* In the basic paradigm for the traditional training group,
the academic research model, adherence to methodology takes
precedence over such other factors as cost, timeliness, or results.
The EOL group uses the "policy research model," whereby *results and timeliness* take precedence over methodology (although
methodology is not unimportant). For example, a decision
maker might say to her staff, "I have to make a decision on this
matter by the end of the week. Let's spend the week learning all
we can so that we can make the best, most-informed decision
possible." The decision maker here isn't concerned so much

Table 8.1. Comparison of traditional training and development groups and employee and organizational learning groups.

	Traditional Training and Development	Employee and Organizational Learning
Basic Paradigm	• Academic research model • Focus on methodology • Reactive service function • People learn through intentional, trainer-designed programs • Trainer-directed	• Policy research model • Focus on business results • Proactive business partner • People learn in many ways, intentional and serendipitous • Learner-directed
Goals	• Excellence measured by strict adherence to methodologies • Transfer of information • Volume (student-weeks)	• Excellence measured by improvement in business results • Creation of knowledge • Just-in-time learning
Focus	• Training workers to continue business as usual • New, innovative programs instituted only when mandated by business leadership	• Improving work methods and business results • Encouraging all employees to innovate, and giving them the tools they need to innovate
Product	• Information	• Knowledge
Evaluation Methods	• Pre-tests and post-tests • Student satisfaction ("smile sheets") • Evaluation measures mastering of information presented in program	• Improved business results, e.g., —Cost reduction —Reduction in defects —Increased profits
Methods	• Formal training programs • Self-paced training (paper- or media-based) • Computer-based training	Traditional programs, *plus* • Individual study • Coaching • Team learning • Benchmarking • Action learning projects • Learning partnerships • Sharing ideas and knowledge (in person and through a knowledge network)
Training Staff and Roles	• Professional educators, trainers, and instructional designers as knowledge resources • External consultants and trainers who meet internal standards	• All company employees as knowledge resources • External resources as needed • Instructional design • Training delivery • Consultation • Coaching • Librarian • Database administrator • Information broker
Company View of Training	• Expense • Time away from the job	• Investment • Integrated with job activities

with the methodology used for learning as with the quality of the decision and the deadline for that decision.

✳ The traditional training organization has as its goal to shape what takes place in the classroom. The EOL group is focused on what happens *on the job*: Will the student be able to apply new knowledge and skills to make a measurable improvement in job performance?

✳ Because the product of the traditional training group is a training program, instructor-led or self-paced, its product can only contain information: data that are relevant to students' work. The EOL group's responsibilities go beyond the learning activity to include *application* of that learning to the employee's work—that is, knowledge rather than information.

✳ Most companies view traditional training activities as an expense that they hope contributes to the bottom line, even when there appears to be little direct connection to it. The knowledge-enabled organization views all learning that is sponsored or facilitated by the EOL group as an *investment* in the future because it has a direct, visible connection to business results.

The bottom line is that the skill set of the traditional training group is still needed by the company, but it must be broadened and put directly into the context of the business. This requires both building a positive learning environment, as already described, and reorienting the traditional training group. One effective way to start this reorientation is to appoint and train an EOL advisory board to provide strategic guidance to the EOL group and, at the same time, act as an advocate for EOL initiatives throughout the company.

Using an Advisory Board as a Strategic Tool

Many traditional training groups try to use an advisory board but have poor experiences with them. I recently spoke with the training director of a large manufacturing company about her organization's advisory board.

"It's pretty worthless," she told me. "When I started in this position two years ago, my manager, the vice-president of human resources, recruited the ten business unit vice-presidents to serve on the advisory board. The first couple of meetings were pretty good, but today we're lucky if five of them show up for any given meeting. We haven't seen several of them for more than a year."

"Can you tell me something about the meetings?" I asked.

"We meet on the first Monday morning of each month. We're supposed to start at 9:30. This gives the members a chance to get in early to check on important messages and such before coming to the meeting. By the time we have everyone here—everyone who is coming, that is—it is usually a little after ten. The afternoon subcommittee meetings are a joke. Half the time, one subcommittee or another has nobody there, and another will have only one person. For all practical purposes, the subcommittees no longer exist."

"What happens at a typical Monday morning meeting?"

"We start off by presenting the statistics for the past month: student hours, ratings, budget data, and so on. Then we talk about any new programs that have rolled out in the past month and any new ones scheduled for the next month."

"Is there any discussion?"

"Once in a while, someone will ask a good question about a new program. Most times, the questions focus on trends in enrollment. They also pay a lot of attention to the budget data—how much we are spending and why. Once in a while, someone will pass along a comment about a particular program from one of their employees."

To my view, this company's advisory board is useless. I don't blame the no-shows, and I wonder why the others bother to come. But it does not have to be this way. The advisory board can be a vital strategic tool for any EOL manager, whether managing a one-person shop or a companywide function with dozens of employees.

Why Have an Advisory Board?

If the EOL group is to play a key role in helping the company and its employees succeed, it must endeavor to fully understand the company's business: strategic business directions, core competencies, competitive challenges, new strategic business initiatives, etc. Whether EOL has one or dozens of employees, it is difficult to keep up with everything that is happening in the company, to understand all aspects of the various businesses, to understand all the competitive issues and pressures. A properly selected advisory board can provide key insights and understanding for the EOL group.

At the same time, the advisory board members can act as key advocates for EOL activities throughout the organization. Advisory board members can become sponsors and champions of key EOL initiatives and can provide pointers to key knowledge resources inside and outside the company. The advisory board can provide key linkages, seeing to it that the company's EOL resources are being utilized to maximum advantage.

Recruiting Members for Your Advisory Board

Who should sit on your company's advisory board? In the vignette just above, the advisory board had very high-level membership: the vice-presidents from the ten major business units. Membership in some advisory boards tends to be focused more on functional lines, with representatives from sales, marketing, engineering, manufacturing, etc. In others, there is a mix of functional and business unit representation. Some companies recruit advisory board members; others call for volunteers.

Business leaders might consider it merely a matter of corporate citizenship to have a representative on the advisory board. "Sure, an advisory board is a good idea," they say, "and I'll appoint someone from my group to be on it." But after making this "commitment," the leader asks the staff, "OK, who has some time available to sit on this board?" without really considering (or caring) who the best representative would be.

I have been asked to do training sessions for several corporate advisory boards and have seen that the people in the room were obviously there because their managers had told them to be there—not from any great interest in the work of the advisory board, or even in the general topic of learning. An advisory board with the wrong membership is at best not useful; at worst, it is a detriment to the achievement of EOL's goals.

To be an effective member of the advisory board, a person should have at least the following qualifications:

* A thorough understanding of the business unit or function she represents. The advisory board member should know how her function or business operates and what its key challenges and core competencies are and be involved in the planning and execution of the function's or unit's strategic business initiatives. The key value that members bring to the advisory board is the ability to help EOL understand the company's business.

* Credibility in the organization. The advisory board member should be a person whose opinion carries weight: "If M— thinks this new program is a good idea, we should give it a chance."

* Time and willingness to help, to work with other advisory board members and with EOL staff for full understanding of the challenges being faced, and to work cooperatively in developing solutions to those challenges.

* A basic understanding of and belief in the value of knowledge and skills in meeting company, organizational, and individual goals. Some advisory boards count within their membership a number of cynics who don't believe that the EOL group can do anything to help the company succeed. Without a reasonable attitude going in, advisory board members cannot be effective—and may end up being dysfunctional.

Some EOL directors feel that the higher the level of the advisory board members, the greater the prestige EOL has in the company. They pressure their own vice-presidents to recruit peers to serve on the board. While an advisory board composed of vice-presidents can be effective, it is more important to ensure that advisory board members meet the criteria given above. Vice-presidents are likely to have many other obligations and not have enough time or energy to devote to the advisory board.

It is also important that the EOL manager personally recruit advisory board members. The personal relationships between the EOL manager and board members are critical. Leaving selection and recruitment of members to, say, a vice-president, misses an important opportunity to build these relationships.

Once you have recruited your advisory board based on these qualifications, you have a good start. But now that you have a board, what do you do with it?

Advisory Board Orientation and Training

Your advisory board is to help EOL better understand the *company's* business. And just as you have been so busy running your EOL group to develop this understanding *yourself*, so advisory board members have been immersed in running their own businesses and have not had time to develop a full understanding of *your* EOL business! Therefore it behooves you, at the initial board meeting, to provide an overview to the EOL function:

* The charter and goals of the EOL group
* An overview of current and planned EOL programs and services
* Current statistics on participation, quality ratings, etc.
* Key internal and external relationships
* Key players from the EOL staff

If EOL in your company has not historically been viewed as a vital contributor to the company's success, share with the board some success stories from other companies that demonstrate how an effective EOL group can add value to strategic business initiatives.

Once the overview is complete, it is time to move on to defining the mission and role of the advisory board itself:

* Why have you asked these people to serve on the board?
* How can EOL help them and the functions/organizations they represent?
* How can they help EOL?
* How should the board function at meetings and between meetings?

Regarding this last point, it is a good idea to present some ideas for ground rules, rather than just throw out the question, sit back, and watch the action. The first meeting should be run by the EOL manager, but the advisory board should elect its own officers and give them responsibility for setting future agendas (with the assistance and advice of the EOL manager, of course).

The board members are quite familiar with the tools and methods they use to plan their own businesses, but they may not know those used by EOL. It serves you well to acquaint them with your methodology; but in doing so, it is vital that you present your methods in a way they understand. It is easy to get so caught up in our own jargon—which makes perfect sense to us—that we fail to recognize it as totally incomprehensible to others who do not share our training and experience.

For example, one company's training director asked me to review a "Training Planning Guide" his group was just completing for use by business unit managers. The guide presented a very comprehensive, systematic planning process that would enable a business manager to start with the business goals, work through a series of steps, and determine the training required for employees to meet those goals. While the guide was very well done, it had two basic problems that doomed it to collect dust on the business managers' bookshelves:

1. It was written in the language of training and development. To a training or human resources professional, it made sense. For a business manager, it was Greek.
2. The planning process detailed in the guide had no relationship to the company's well-established business planning processes. If I were a business manager reading the guide, my reaction would be: "I've just finished

months of work developing plans using the company guidelines, and now you're telling me I have to start over from scratch just to determine training needs? You're crazy!"

A vital task you can undertake with your advisory board is first to develop your own understanding of the business planning processes and then work with the board to extend those processes to determine the learning needed to achieve company, organizational, and individual goals. When the advisory board realizes that EOL is not trying to reinvent the wheel but is only trying to add value to the business (their businesses), the board becomes a powerful strategic tool for helping EOL achieve its own goals.

At the initial orientation and training meeting for the advisory board, it is also wise to select a high-priority company need on which you can focus your initial efforts. For example, is one division trying to implement TQM, introduce a new product line, improve customer service ratings, or move to concurrent engineering? Ask the board to help select one high-priority area that you can work on together to test the planning methodology and, at the same time, demonstrate that EOL really can add value to the company's strategic business initiatives. A quick, effective response to this type of need goes a long way to establishing (or reestablishing) the credibility of your EOL group within the company.

Running the Advisory Board

The advisory board should convene regularly, perhaps quarterly. Depending on the urgency of the items on the agenda, the board may at times need to meet as frequently as once a month. But remember that this is an advisory board, not a management group. In the earlier example, it was ludicrous to think that the ten senior business unit managers would take a full day each month to devote to the advisory board (and the first Monday of the month at that!).

This does not mean that *the work* of the advisory board only comes up four times a year. If convinced that it can add value to the company through its work, the board may appoint its own subcommittees and work steadily on key issues, outside the quarterly meetings. The EOL manager should also provide board members with monthly updates on key issues and programs and should feel free to call on members for advice or assistance as needed. At the same time, board members should call on the EOL manager for assistance in program planning, to advise of changes in priorities or upcoming strategic programs to which EOL can add value, etc.

Each quarterly meeting should be well planned by the board chairperson and the EOL manager to ensure that the meeting time is well utilized and that members feel that their time at the meetings is worthwhile. The typical agenda items of reviewing enrollment statistics, knowledge network usage, budgets, and quality data should be handled in written reports delivered to advisory board members before the meetings; little value is added to the EOL function or to the contribution of the board members by sitting and looking at tables of statistics and listening to someone reading them off the charts.

A properly constituted, properly run advisory board can be a strategic tool for EOL directors seeking to make their organizations key contributors to their company's success. The board can both help revitalize a traditional training group endeavoring to change its focus to employee and organizational learning and become an advocate for the work of the new EOL group.

9

The Learning Organization, the Corporate University, and the Knowledge-Enabled Organization

The learning organization can mean two things; it can mean an organization which learns and/or an organization which encourages learning in its people. It should mean both.

Charles Handy, *The Age of Unreason*

As with other professions, the training field is subject to many trends that are featured monthly in the major training publications and are the subject of many conferences and workshops. In recent years, two of the hottest topics have been the *learning organization*, a term popularized by MIT's Peter Senge, and the *corporate university*. This chapter will examine these two trends and relate them to the model of the knowledge-enabled organization.

The Learning Organization

MIT's Peter Senge, in his book *The Fifth Discipline: The Art and Practice of the Learning Organization* and, subsequently, *The Fifth Discipline Fieldbook*, describes a set of five disciplines. Together these disciplines enable a company to become a *learning organization*, which Senge defines as "an organization that is continually expanding its capacity to create its future."[1] His five disciplines are:

1. Personal mastery
2. Mental models
3. Shared vision
4. Team learning
5. Systems thinking

The learning organization is a hot topic among training professionals, if only because of its name and the obvious connection between "learning" and "training." Senge is also a noted academic, and, as I stated earlier, the training world is very much attached to the academic research model. So Senge's academic research as well as his metaphors, which range from the discipline of systems thinking to the language of "tribes of northern Natal in South Africa," make many training professionals feel very much at home with his conceptual framework and his five disciplines.

But Senge was neither the first nor the last to use the term *learning organization* nor is his the only relevant definition. The knowledge-enabled organization is certainly a learning organization (with or without the explicit use of Senge's five disciplines), one where all employees are using their knowledge, skills, and learning to meet today's business challenges and to create new opportunities for the future.

The five disciplines can be valuable tools, but are not sufficient, in and of themselves, to create a knowledge-enabled organization.

The five tools can be very useful to the knowledge-enabled organization, but they alone are not sufficient to make the knowledge-enabled organization a reality. As is the case with many academics, Senge's methods and examples deal more with theory than application, more with how companies can use the tools than with specific business changes that may result from their use.

The five disciplines are what I call "high-level super-structure"—they are useful, but they must be built on strong foundations of proactive planning, the valuing of employees' knowledge and skills, and the creation of a positive learning environment. With strong foundations in place, the five disciplines can provide some very useful and effective tools. Without strong foundations, the tools may be interesting and fun to use, but they are unlikely to result in measurable gains for the organization. Let's briefly examine each of the five disciplines and how they relate to the model of the knowledge-enabled organization.

1. Senge defines *personal mastery* as the "discipline of personal growth and learning."[2] He states that it is not just gaining more information, but using that information to produce results. In the knowledge-enabled organization, this is ultimately reflected in the learning contract, where every learning goal is tied directly to a business goal and includes measures of expected results.

2. The second discipline, *mental models,* is vital to any change effort. By making our mental models explicit, we uncover the assumptions on which our thinking, planning, and actions are based. Too often, companies and individuals work on hidden agendas where underlying assumptions are either deliberately hidden or the status quo is taken as a given—in either case, these assumptions may become formidable roadblocks to progress. By using the discipline of mental models, we can get those assumptions out in the open, examine them, and see whether they make sense or should be abandoned. Mental models can also be a very useful tool in helping employees transform their tacit knowledge into explicit knowledge.

A project team from a graduate management program undertook a project for a senior manager in a manufacturing company. The manager was stymied by her inability to get her organization to change the way it worked. The project team used a set of tools to detail the mental models being used by this manager and her direct reports in addressing the change program. When the work was done, the team presented the results to the manager: "We have found the roadblock."

"Great!" said the manager enthusiastically. "What is it?"

"It's you," reported the team leader. "For years, you have been telling your team that the company wouldn't even consider buying new equipment. And this change effort you are trying to undertake absolutely requires some new capital investment."

"But I am open to prudent capital investment. The freeze on capital expenditures was taken off about eighteen months ago," replied the manager.

"You never told your people that. They're still operating under the assumption that no capital spending will be allowed. They remember how you used to rage at them for even suggesting that capital investment was needed. And they can't come up with a solution to the problem without that capital investment."

"I'm glad to hear that the problem is me," said the manager. "I can change me."

3. *Shared vision,* Senge's third discipline, is also vital to the knowledge-enabled organization and is reflected in its definition of the organizational vision and the alignment of all parts of the organization with that vision. As is often said, if you don't know where you are going, any road will do. A shared vision provides everyone in the organization with a common destination.

4. *Team learning,* discipline number four, describes a set of practices and tools for helping people to work more effectively as members of a team. I totally agree. For me, the only reason to ever assemble a team is to enable team members to learn from each other and to learn together how to optimize a business process.

5. Finally, *systems thinking,* Senge's fifth discipline—the one that dominates the discussion within his book—is another method for understanding how an organization's business processes really work and how various parts of those processes interact with and affect one another. This approach is paralleled in the knowledge-enabled organization when all employees, at all levels, develop an understanding of the business processes of which their work is a part and of how individual and group work contributes to the overall goals of the company. In the knowledge-enabled organization, systems thinking may be used at a higher conceptual level to start employees thinking about how different parts of the organization relate to one another. Process mapping may be used at a more detailed level to help employees understand the specific relationships among actual work processes.

So, if Senge's learning organization so parallels the knowledge-enabled organization, why do we need another book? Why not just tell everyone to read and implement *The Fifth Discipline*? I have argued throughout this book that training professionals, in order to gain credibility in their companies and to become part of the mainstream efforts to achieve the company's goals, must learn their companies' businesses and business vocabulary and must integrate their own goals with those of the company. Senge's book does not talk the language of the business, but relies more on academic jargon and dialectic.

The Fifth Discipline has sold hundreds of thousands of copies. I would conjecture that fewer than 10 percent of the people who bought the book have actually read the entire text. And, from those who made it all the way through, a remark I commonly heard was: "Well, the man is obviously brilliant. He has a lot of good ideas. But what am I supposed to do?"

Perhaps in response to this type of comment, Senge and several of his colleagues published *The Fifth Discipline Fieldbook*[3] several years after the first book. This book, which contains many short articles by Senge, his MIT colleagues, and business and consulting practitioners, offers many examples of how to use each of the five disciplines and some case studies of their application in real business situations. But again, the fieldbook falls short in providing a practical approach to building a learning organization.

> Over the past several years, I have been contacted by a number of potential clients about helping them become "learning organizations." When I talked with them and asked what they meant by the term *learning organization*, none of them could clearly articulate what they meant, other than to say: "We need to learn how to change, how to become better at what we do. Isn't that what a learning organization is?"

The Knowledge-Enabled Organization has been designed to provide more practical advice, many real-world examples, and a comprehensive approach to using individual and organizational learning, and the resultant knowledge and skills, to enable the transformation or renewal of your company. So, what should you do with Senge's five disciplines? The answer is that they provide a set of valuable tools that should become part of the "toolbox" of the Employee and Organizational Learning Group and be used appropriately. The knowledge-enabled organization should have a wide variety of learning methods and tools, *including* Senge's, within its repertoire to meet whatever learning need arises. The effectiveness of the knowledge-enabled organization is derived from how well it selects the appropriate tool or method for each of those learning needs.

The Corporate University

By recent estimates, several thousand U.S. companies have created corporate universities, colleges, or institutes to meet the learning needs of their employees. One of the earliest and most noted of these ventures is Motorola University, but the trend crosses all industries and companies of all sizes. I would argue that this trend is more of a naming convention than a real change in the way in which companies are addressing the learning needs of their employees.

Establishing a corporate university does not guarantee that there will be any change in the way the corporation's employees are trained.

Why would a company want to create a corporate university? There are several reasons. First, company leaders may really believe that knowledge and skills will form the basis of future competitive advantage for the company and may be ready to make an investment in establishing a corporate university as the means to further employee development in those areas.

Second, it may sound impressive to customers or partners when the CEO can say that "our people are trained in our own university" or "if we sign this partnership agreement, we can also open the doors of our university to your employees."

Third, if the impetus for establishing the corporate university is coming directly from an existing training organization, the training group may be pushing for greater recognition and resources. After all, most of the prestige that comes from establishing a corporate university falls to the former training group. Once the "training group" or "training department" that reported to a human resources-vice president, it is now the "corporate university" reporting to the company president or chief operating officer. "I used to be a training manager, now I'm a dean!"

Some real benefits to the company's training efforts, especially from the view of the training group, may accompany this prestige:

✳ When a company establishes a corporate university, the company's CEO and other high-level executives generally become more directly involved in the training effort. How long this direct involvement lasts will depend on what benefits they see to the company and to themselves from their participation.

✳ Establishing a corporate university usually means that training budgets will increase and, perhaps, that an actual campus will be built. From the view of the training director or dean, these can be great benefits.

✳ The corporate university creates a new and increased focus on training and on how training can make the company and its employees more productive. Where training had previously been taken for granted ("Yes, we do some training for our employees"), the new university creates more dialogue about the role of training in helping to meet company goals.

Several years ago, I gave a keynote presentation for a national conference on corporate universities. I entitled the presentation: "If The Corporate University Is the Answer, What's the Question?" The point of the presentation was that transforming the training group into a corporate university does not guarantee that the company's training efforts will be any more effective in helping the company and its employees meet their collective and individual goals than they were before the university was established. In fact, the establishment of a corporate university can be detrimental to the goals of the knowledge-enabled organization. How?

✳ When a company establishes a university, and especially when it moves training operations to a separate campus, it isolates the training group from the real world of the company's business. In the knowledge-enabled organization, the goal is to get training professionals (or learning facilitators, to use my new term) more directly involved in the company's business, not to separate them from it.

✳ The corporate university gives line managers an even greater excuse to ignore their own responsibilities for the learning needs of their employees. "That's why we established this university—that's where people go to learn. Now I can concentrate on my real work." In the knowledge-enabled organization, managers at all levels take responsibility for facilitating their employees' learning (and their own) to meet individual, group, and company goals—that *is* their real work.

✳ Giving the company's training efforts the title "university" almost ensures that its staff will be even more closely tied to the academic research model. As discussed in Chapter 1, this model tends to separate the university staff even more from the realities of the business world. "Now that we're a university, we must be even more careful about following strict methodologies for design and delivery of our curriculum to meet the academic standards implied by our new name."

Given the above caveats, I remain neutral on whether companies should create corporate universities. But, in examining the work of real academic universities, I believe that there are some ideas from academia that could be profitably adapted to the corporate setting. These include:

* The university research agenda
* Visiting professors
* The university extension service
* Community service
* Student internships

The University Research Agenda

The job description of every academic university professor includes a research component. The goal of this research is generally to add knowledge to his or her field of specialization, to develop and test new theories and methods, and, as they are tested, to add the new knowledge to the curriculum.

In most corporate settings, instructors spend the bulk of their time teaching—hours accrued in the classroom and student-days taught are standard measures of productivity in corporate training. But corporate faculty should also be engaging in research, both basic and applied.

* *Basic* research focuses on laws and corollaries—biologists engaged in basic research strive to understand how biological systems work (for example, the human genome project, where scientists are trying to uncover the human genetic code). For corporate faculty members, basic research focuses on developing a better understanding of the content of their curriculum. For example, a trainer focused on TQM courses might develop an improved understanding of the sciences of statistics and measurement.

✳ *Applied* research focuses on knowledge that can be directly related to the student's work. Corporate faculty should spend time observing the work of their students on the job. Unless faculty members understand the work their students are doing, they cannot make the classes relevant to that work. Unless they understand the challenges facing the student on the job, they cannot design instruction to help them meet the employees' and the company's goals. Unless they leave their ivory towers occasionally, they will never see if what they are recommending to students actually pertains to their day-to-day employment tasks and responsibilities.

Both types of faculty research are necessary for the knowledge-enabled organization to succeed. Basic research enables faculty members to identify, understand, and utilize the best information available, inside or outside the company, and to design learning activities for employees who need to use that information. Applied research makes the faculty more effective in transforming that information into knowledge, thus helping to ensure that the information is applied to students' work to make positive differences in individual and company performance. Unfortunately, many training groups today tend to ignore the learning needs of their own staff members and, where learning opportunities are provided, tend to focus narrowly on instructional design techniques (for example, developing intranet-based training programs) rather than on the company's business.

Visiting Professors

Along with regular, full-time faculty, universities often utilize visiting professors—professors who come from other universities to serve on the faculty for a short term, typically a year. Sometimes the visiting professor is not a regular academic, but an "executive-in-residence" or "artist-in-residence" who comes to share his or her knowledge with students and faculty and, at the same time, learn from them.

The idea of visiting faculty is one that could also serve the corporation well. For example, when I managed a technical curriculum for a high-tech company, we continually had difficulty hiring qualified instructors. Employees in the training group had lower pay scales than those in real-world, hands-on positions within the company. We also didn't offer the perquisites that many field-based jobs offered, such as company cars and expense accounts. (This relative undervaluing of corporate training personnel is a separate issue that I won't deal with here.) At the same time, when I talked with field supervisors, they told me that fully 50 percent of their time was spent in doing on-the-job training of newly hired personnel. My solution: If first-line supervisors had major responsibilities for on-the-job training, why not require candidates for these supervisory positions to spend a year in the corporate training group? This would help the company by:

* Alleviating the shortage of qualified instructors in the corporate training group.
* Ensuring that the instructors who were training new hires for field-based positions had real-world experience in those positions. These visiting professors could also have a great positive effect on the curriculum for the new hires since they themselves had been doing the jobs for which they were preparing their students.
* Better preparing new first-line supervisors for their on-the-job training responsibilities, and making their supervisory jobs easier because they would know exactly what training the new hires had been receiving.

I also believe that many other subject-matter experts within the company should rotate through the training function, or employee and organizational learning group, as visiting professors.

* Executives who teach classes not only emphasize the importance of the curriculum by their very presence ("if a corporate vice-president is teaching this course, it must be important"), but they also tend to learn a lot about what is happening down in the trenches by listening to students (employees) with whom they would normally have no contact. This has certainly

been the experience of Amoco executives who participate in the programs of the Amoco Management Learning Center.

＊ Subject-matter experts from all levels of the company can typically provide more up-to-date information to students than even the best-prepared full-time instructors. Full-time faculty members spend most of their time in the classroom and don't have the same recent real-world experience as do subject-matter experts who take time from their regular jobs to act as instructors. In addition, when the training is completed, the subject-matter experts, back in their old jobs, can also provide on-the-job coaching and reinforcement of newly learned information and newly acquired skills—something full-time faculty members typically cannot do because they are already busy teaching the next class. The very successful AMP Engineering Education Program is built on the principle of always using subject-matter experts as instructors. AMP has found that this practice also helps to reinforce the company's engineering culture and build informal networks among students and faculty that also promote learning on the job.

＊ Just as executives and subject-matter experts should spend time in the classroom, full-time instructors should spend time working in noninstructional positions. When instructors have done the work they are teaching their students to do, they gain credibility with the students and learn more about the real-world situations that students face daily in their work.

The University Extension Service

State-funded land-grant universities have long traditions of providing extension services to the agricultural community (and more recently to the business and manufacturing communities). The purpose of these extension services is to take knowledge from the university directly out to the people who can use it to improve their farms and businesses. Extension services include instructing, consulting, and disseminating information.

The corporate university, or the employee and organizational learning group, should similarly perform extension services. Faculty members, or learning facilitators, cannot just sit in their offices waiting for people to come to them. When they have information that can help the business, they should proactively share that information throughout the company, as described here:

* Through the knowledge network, faculty members can share new ideas from their research and from their classroom experiences. If a new technique seems to be working well in the classroom, the instructor can make it known to a wider audience by posting information about that technique on the knowledge network.
* By consulting with managers and employees all over the company, faculty members can bring their knowledge directly into the business without having to wait for people to sign up for a course.
* By making presentations to work groups, instructors can provide just-in-time, just-enough learning opportunities to those groups.
* By regularly meeting with various groups—for example, by attending quarterly status meetings—faculty members can gain a better understanding of the real-world problems faced by the company. With this knowledge, they can design better solutions to learning problems, suggest solutions that already exist but which are not well known, or find applied research sites to help employees develop new solutions.

Community Service

In most universities, faculty members are measured on their teaching, research, and community service activities. Community service focuses on service both to the university and to the general community. Serving the university means becoming involved in faculty committees, department meetings, and college and university planning committees. Corporate university instructors should similarly become more actively involved in the overall business issues of their companies. They should serve on planning committees and on benchmarking teams and should represent the company to external constituencies. The benefits from such community service include the following:

* Many trainers today feel isolated from the rest of the company; serving on cross-functional teams or committees involves training personnel in the wider issues of the company and helps them to overcome their own personal and functional myopia.
* Training personnel who actively participate in planning for the company's future add value by identifying knowledge and skill requirements and learning methods that will help the company's plans succeed. In more forward-looking companies, no planning effort—whether for a new plant, a new product, or a new program—can be approved without a learning plan in place.

Student Internships

Many academic universities help students find internships through which they can learn more about the real world, start testing their knowledge and skills, and integrate their classroom learning with real-world work. Internships are but one of many learning methods that should be used in companies to help develop employees' knowledge and skills. They are especially important in the transmission of tacit knowledge—knowledge held by practitioners that is not easily translatable into the classroom.

The Learning Organization, the Corporate University, and the Knowledge-Enabled Organization

The learning organization, the corporate university, and the knowledge-enabled organization are not mutually exclusive terms. A knowledge-enabled organization will certainly exhibit all or most of the characteristics of the learning organization as defined by Senge. But I believe that introducing Senge's five disciplines is not, in and of itself, sufficient to produce a knowl-edge-enabled organization.

Similarly, creating a corporate university does not preclude the development of a knowledge-enabled organization. As I stated earlier, I consider the corporate university primarily a naming convention. Whether you call it the corporate university or the employee and organizational learning group is not as im-portant as how you define the work of the group. If the corpo-rate university follows the guidelines presented throughout this book, and especially in Chapter 8, there is no reason why the company cannot become a knowledge-enabled organization.

Notes

1. Peter Senge, *The Fifth Discipline: The Art and Practice of the Learning Organization* (New York: Doubleday/Currency, 1990), p. 14.
2. Ibid., p. 141.
3. Peter Senge, Art Kleiner, Charlotte Roberts, Richard B. Ross, and Bryan J. Smith, *The Fifth Discipline Fieldbook* (New York: Currency/ Doubleday, 1994).

10

Moving Learning Beyond Company Boundaries

The effective executive has to be able to recognize and run with opportunity, to learn, and constantly to refresh the knowledge base.

Peter Drucker, *Managing for the Future*
Truman Talley/Dutton

Most of the learning resources a company needs already exist within its own boundaries. But there are times when learning activities have to extend beyond those boundaries. If your company requires more knowledge and skills, you have three basic strategies:

1. You can buy knowledge and skills.
2. You can rent them.
3. You can develop them.

Most of this book has involved the third choice. It is time to consider the other two knowledge-acquisition strategies.

Buying Knowledge and Skills

The quickest way to fill deficits in specific knowledge and skills may be to buy the necessary resources. You can do this by hiring people who already have the necessary knowledge and skills. The tens of thousands of job advertisements appearing in newspapers all the time represent attempts to buy knowledge and skills on the open market.

An alternative is to acquire or merge with another company with complementary specialized knowledge and skills. Microsoft, for example, has bought a number of small companies to benefit its business strategies in the Internet area.

Companies also buy knowledge by subscribing to external services that collect information on various technical, market, and management trends. "Industry watchers"—companies such as the Gartner Group and the International Data Group (IDG)— offer subscriptions with periodic reports on trends in the information technology and telecommunications markets. Coopers & Lybrand's Tax News Network lets customers access the latest tax-related news, for a fee.

The buy strategy makes sense when a business determines that developing the needed knowledge and skills internally will cost too much, in terms of dollars or time—that is, when the learning need is immediate and the learning curve is too steep for current employees, when compared with the urgency of responding to market pressures.

Renting Knowledge and Skills

Companies *rent* knowledge and skills when their learning need is temporary. For example, in designing a product, there may be a call for specialized knowledge to select the packaging material. If the company does not have the necessary knowledge to do this within its current workforce, it may hire a consultant to help make this one-time decision, or subcontract the problem to a company whose sole business is product packaging. In either case, the company rents the needed knowledge on a short-term basis to meet an immediate need.

How can you find the external knowledge resources to pursue a rent strategy? Odds are your office is inundated with queries from potential consultants and vendors offering to share their expertise with your company. All of this information should become part of the company's knowledge database:

* What consultants, subcontractors, and vendors are available?
* What products or services do they provide?
* What has been the company's experience with them?

This type of database is most often found in the purchasing or procurement function, but it should be made available to all employees, first so they can more easily find the external resources they need and second so they can add information to the database. Employees also learn about external resources when they attend conferences, take outside courses, and talk with friends and colleagues in other companies. This type of information could easily remain with the individual employee who develops it or, at best, within the employee's area. Again, this is where sharing knowledge benefits everyone. One employee or group spends many hours or days trying to find an external knowledge resource, not knowing that another group has already found and used a consultant or vendor who would have a perfect solution for them.

Finding external knowledge resources is itself a new industry. Knowledge brokers take responsibility for developing networks of experts and information sources for their clients. One of the most successful of this new type of company is Minneapolis-based Teltech.

Knowledge Broker Teltech

University of Texas business school professor Tom Davenport describes Teltech's business as "helping companies get access to external technical expertise and information."[1] Teltech's business provides four key services to a wide variety of technology companies:

1. An expert network encompasses thousands of experts in technical fields. "When a client calls Teltech," Davenport says, "they engage in a dialogue with a Teltech 'knowl-

edge analyst' about their problem, or they are given one
or more names of experts who can speak knowledgeably
on the customer's issue."[2]

2. Teltech provides its clients with access to more than sixteen hundred online databases, with searches assisted by
knowledge analysts.

3. A vendor search service finds vendors for specific technical products and services. This client service includes locating and qualifying potential vendors.

4. A technical alert service provides weekly technical
briefings on significant research developments worldwide.

In these ways, Teltech serves as a prime knowledge resource
for its member companies, allowing them to identify and locate
knowledge resources beyond their own boundaries.

Along with identifying and hiring expert consultants, companies also turn to short-term, expert contract employees as a
way to meet knowledge and skills requirements.

Using Contract Employees

The temporary employment industry is changing its focus from
unskilled and office jobs to high-level technical and managerial
jobs. This has resulted from the downsizing trend in American
industry: Companies that have drastically reduced the number
of professional positions find that their reductions in force have
left them short of key skills. "Why should we keep all of these
professionals on staff," employers wonder, "when we don't
need them all the time?" Contract personnel fill just-in-time,
just-enough requirements for specific knowledge and skills. At
the same time, as tens of thousands of highly skilled technical
and professional employees who have entered the labor market
find that there are few full-time positions for them, they turn to
short-term contract assignments to make their livelihood.

How are companies using these interim employees? A
writer for *Industry Week* online gives these examples:

* Sheffield Steel hired a quality expert to implement the
changes necessary to get its plants . . . ISO 9000-certified.

* A small start-up company with seven people—but none with marketing skills—brought in a marketing expert for three months to develop and initiate a strategy for a hot product it had developed.
* When Sara Lee Intimates merged two operating divisions, it hired an experienced chief financial officer who, in less than five months, identified best practices, designed a new financial structure, and established a realistic time frame for implementation.[3]

Many companies find that this a very cost-effective method to meet interim needs for specific knowledge and skills. For example:

A detergent manufacturer that makes its own bottles paid twice the normal salary when it needed two people who could operate blow-molding equipment—a skill that takes three years to learn and fifteen to become an expert—for less than a year. "We could have moved a few people out of another of our plants or subcontracted the work out," says a company representative. "But you are talking about $5–10 million a year versus $100,000 to pay interim workers."[4]

How Companies Use, Buy, and Rent Strategies

If a company feels it needs some specific knowledge on a long-term basis, it can either hire someone with the necessary knowledge (the buy strategy) or develop the knowledge by training existing employees while renting the knowledge for the interim until its own employees are trained. In such a case, it may also use a hybrid rent/develop strategy, hiring a consultant to meet the immediate need but ask that consultant to train employees to do it themselves in the longer term.

Companies using buy and rent knowledge-acquisition strategies move their learning strategies beyond the boundaries. But these are not the only ways to move learning beyond company boundaries. Another major learning strategy is to learn from customers.

Learning From Your Customers

Whether you are in a product or a service business, your customers should be the ones determining what the company produces. This reflects a growing move from producing the state of the art to producing the "state of the need." Engineers frequently create products that use the latest in technology even if those are not what the customer needs. Unless the company understands the customer's needs, unless it learns the business and how the customer uses its products and services, it cannot effectively meet those needs. Writing in *Industry Week*, John Mariotti states, "For technology choices to be truly effective, the users must have some input. . . . Most managers simply are not familiar with enough details at the user level, and engineers often select sophisticated solutions that go far beyond practical needs."[5] Mariotti's view is reinforced by another writer for *Industry Week*, who quotes consultant Mike Anthony:

> Anthony says that the more high-tech a company is, the worse it seems to be at defining products early on. "What happens is that someone's got a great idea for a neat, sexy piece of technology and wants to embed that in a new product or come up with a new product, but what they don't really think about is the whole market side: How would someone use this product? How would you articulate the benefit to the customer?"[6]

Ignoring the customer is a sure way to create products and services that don't sell. Learning from customers before designing solutions to their problems is the right way to ensure that your products and services will sell.

IBM Research has learned this lesson. According to vice-president Armando Garcia,

> We do it by forging a more direct connection with the marketplace. So in many ways we've opened up the

doors to our laboratories to let our customers reach in and tell us about their business problems. They tell us where their industry segment is going, and we share where we see technology moving—in their sector as well as others. The idea is to connect directly with their problems and devise first-of-a-kind solutions.[7]

Just as companies must understand their own business processes, they must also understand the processes within their customers' businesses when their products or services are part of those processes. This type of learning allows a company to become more than just a commodity supplier; it becomes an integral part of the customer's business, an enviable and productive relationship that ensures long-term customer satisfaction and loyalty. Many large companies have changed their purchasing procedures from always selecting the low-cost producer to one where they partner with suppliers. This trend has allowed small suppliers to benefit from long-term relationships with their larger customers. At Ace Clearwater Enterprises, a small, Southern California sheet-metal fabricator, learning from customers has become a way of life and has paid great dividends.

Learning From Customers at Ace Clearwater Enterprises

Ace Clearwater Enterprises (ACE) has doubled its annual revenue from $10 million to $20 million over the past two years. Its learning strategies, using a combination of buying, renting, and developing the knowledge and skills it needed for this growth, have almost doubled revenue with virtually no increase in total employment.

ACE's customer list includes major aerospace and industrial companies Boeing, AlliedSignal Aerospace, Lockheed, and GE Power Generation. By listening and learning, ACE has become a preferred supplier to all of these large customers. While ACE still sells to these customers, they also bring new business directly to ACE. For example, based on the excellent experience its U.S. operations have had in working with ACE, GE's Power

Generation division has asked ACE to become a major supplier to its partially owned subsidiaries in India.

ACE learns from its customers in several ways:

* The company conducts annual customer surveys, asking "What do we do well? What do we do poorly? What do we need to learn?"
* Its employees attend workshops that customers such as Boeing and AlliedSignal put on for their suppliers.
* It integrates systems with customers; for example, by signing onto McDonnell Douglas's World Wide Web page, ACE employees can access the latest specifications and engineering change orders for parts they are producing without having to wait for paperwork to be sent through the various channels at McDonnell and ACE.
* But mostly, according to ACE CEO Kellie Dodson and vice-president Gary Johnson, "We learn by listening to the customer."

ACE has also participated heavily in training programs offered through the California Supplier Improvement Program (CALSIP), which is sponsored by a consortium of large aerospace and defense companies and designed to improve the quality of the products and services those prime contractors receive from their networks of small suppliers.

This learning does not just flow to companies from their customers. It also moves from suppliers to customers. As ACE develops expertise in sheet-metal fabrication, it also teaches customers how to design parts for better manufacturability. Many of ACE's customers have come to rely upon the company's specialized expertise and buy not just parts from ACE but also its knowledge of fabrication. One customer recently said, "You know how to produce these parts better than we could ever do. Let us buy the equipment you need to produce a new line of parts for us. We could set up the production facilities ourselves, but we would never be able to match your knowledge and experience in making these types of parts." Even though these aerospace giants have greater overall expertise and many more resources, they rely on ACE for specialized knowledge and skills.

Tying Customers Into Your Company's Knowledge Network

Some companies give key customers access to their knowledge networks. For example, Buckman Laboratories has created "customer forums" through which they can ask questions and hold discussions directly with Buckman personnel. As with many of these efforts, Buckman separates the forums from their internal systems and uses a "fire wall" to keep customers and others from accessing proprietary company databases.

The makers of many computer hardware and software products host forums on major public services, such as CompuServe, America Online, and the Microsoft Network, to allow customers to seek answers to their questions and problems either by searching databases of known problems and solutions or by asking questions in discussion forums. These questions may be answered by company personnel or by other users.

Many companies tie their own computer systems to those of their customers and suppliers to practice just-in-time manufacturing and inventory control. The exchange of information yields great improvements for all parties in inventory costs, manufacturing schedules, and order lead times. In essence, they are all learning from each other—learning to control costs and processes to benefit all of the involved parties.

The knowledge-enabled organization also learns from customers, suppliers, and even competitors— from any and every relevant source within or without the company.

Moving From Sharing Knowledge to Selling Knowledge

As your company builds knowledge-sharing relationships with your customers and suppliers, you may find that there is additional value you can add, and sell, to them. When supermarkets started using electronic scanners at their checkout counters, the original intent was to keep better track of their own inventories. Over time, they discovered that the information they collected had value to their suppliers, and they began selling the information to both their immediate suppliers and, further down the value chain, to food producers.

General Electric built a relationship with health care giant Columbia/HCA Healthcare Corp., selling them CAT scanners, magnetic resonance imagers, and other medical equipment for more than three hundred hospitals. As the relationship between the two companies developed, GE negotiated a contract to service all of the hospital chain's imaging equipment, regardless of manufacturer. But that was not the end of the relationship. As reported in *Business Week:*

> As the new contract evolved, Columbia executives invited a team of GE managers to help improve the way they run hospitals. GE is now providing Columbia with a big dose of its well-known management skills. From GE's fabled "workouts" to seminars on supply-chain management and employee training, GE execs are working with Columbia to boost productivity.
>
> For Columbia, which has saved tens of millions of dollars, it was medicine well worth swallowing. But for GE, the benefits go well beyond added revenue. The open-ended relationship is a smart gambit to gain a greater lock on one of its biggest customers.[8]

Through this relationship, Jack Welch opens up GE to a whole new line of business, using the knowledge it has developed in its own businesses to gain a greater lock on key customers and also to provide a new revenue stream based on that knowledge.

Similarly, Buckman Laboratories uses the knowledge developed in serving key industries (such as pulp and paper) to sell consulting services, in addition to its chemicals, to those industries. The knowledge that Buckman has acquired in years of working with specific industries has value over and above the specialty chemicals it produces; it yields a new, growing line of revenue.

Learning From and With Competitors and Others

Many companies regularly buy their competitors' products so that they can study and learn from them. Automobile manufacturers buy their competitors' models. When I worked for Digital Equipment, I once met the sales representative who sold to IBM. "They're one of our best customers," the rep told me. "They buy one of everything we make."

When specialized learning needs arise and companies cannot find learning resources within their own boundaries or from available external sources, they sometimes form consortia so they can learn together. In the United Kingdom, one such learning consortium is the Management Forum for Excellence in Software Development. According to one of its cofounders, David Bell, the forum includes companies ranging from Motorola to British Telecom and Reuters. While many of the forum members sell competing products and services, they have come together to learn with and from each other about how to manage the process of software development by[9]:

* Sharing practical experience: "Put the lessons of other managers to best effect in your own organizations."
* Providing practical help: "Set strategic improvement goals. Design and implement effective improvement activities. Make significant and lasting gains in performance, quality, and productivity."
* Increasing confidence: "Start improvement initiatives knowing that they have already produced valuable results. Obtain practical help through the Forum if progress heads in unexpected directions."
* Providing richness of input: "Members represent many types of organizations and market areas."
* Focus on practical and new ideas: "Better manage your

software product and system development, and software procurement."

There are also many learning consortia based at universities in the United States, among them the Leaders for Manufacturing program at MIT and the Center for Agile Manufacturing at Lehigh University. These university-based centers provide the latest research and learning from the universities as well as learning opportunities for their members, both from university faculty and from the companies themselves. Rather than rely on courses and programs that universities publish in their catalogs, consortium membership allows companies to specify their learning needs and to have custom learning opportunities created for them by university faculty.

Another method for learning from others' experience, whether direct competitors or companies in completely different industries, is through benchmarking. Benchmarking is simply the study of how other companies do things—handle customer service, communicate with their employees, design new products, market their services, and so forth. By studying the experiences of other companies, you can learn from others' successes while avoiding errors they have made. Benchmarking can be done by visiting other companies, or by studying their operations through reading previous studies. Several industry and professional groups have developed benchmark clearinghouses to collect and disseminate studies already done and to identify appropriate benchmark sites for their members.

Using the Knowledge Network to Share External Knowledge

Whenever your company does or buys a benchmark study, that information should also be deposited in your knowledge repository. A manufacturing plant, for example, might conduct benchmark studies on a given topic, such as implementing statistical process control, and never share it beyond the walls of the plant. Later, another plant in the same company wants to develop its own approach to SPC, never knowing that the first plant has already conducted those benchmarks. So the second plant wastes a lot of money doing its own studies and delays implementation of SPC while the unnecessary studies are done. Sharing of benchmark information through the knowledge network can avoid these costly duplications of effort. Knowledge is a unique economic good: You can give it away and still keep it.

Every employee in a company continuously gathers information from both internal and external sources, but most of this information is never shared with others. Consider some of the ways in which employees learn from external sources, and how that information could benefit others in the company:

✳ A quality manager attending an industry conference hears many speakers, collects papers and studies, sees displays of new products, and meets consultants who are selling their own unique services and approaches. Some of this information makes an impact on the employee, and so she retains it. But many others in the company, in and outside of her immediate group, can also benefit from some of that information. By writing a summary report and placing it in a discussion forum, she sparks the interest of other employees. By placing papers in the corporate library, and placing pointers to those papers in the appropriate discussion forums or bulletin boards, she makes the information available to still others. Her information about other companies' experiences (as reported at the conference) in appropriate files in the knowledge network helps identify benchmark targets as well as potential subcontractors. Information on consultants at the conference helps yet others locate consulting assistance they need.

✳ Usually, an engineer reads the magazines and journals he receives and either tosses them out or puts them on a shelf to collect dust. Using the knowledge network, relevant articles can be scanned into the corporate library database and pointers can direct workers to topics in journals that now remain at hand.

✳ As a member of a professional society or subscriber to industry or professional periodicals, a trainer receives many notices of meetings, courses, workshops, and symposia. Typically, they are thrown out as junk mail, or possibly notices are posted on the office bulletin board. If, instead, the trainer places these notices on the knowledge network's bulletin boards or in the appropriate discussion forums, others not on the same mailing lists might benefit from finding a seminar they have been seeking.

  * Attending a trade show, a marketing specialist gathers a lot of competitive information. Rather than just sharing the information with members of her own group, she places it in the appropriate discussion forums for wider dissemination.

  * In handling a phone order, a call center representative hears the customer say, "I know that your XYZ model is designed for this use, but we have also found it very valuable in doing ABC." This type of information on a possible new use is generally lost. Using the knowledge network, the call center rep places the customer's remark in the appropriate discussion forum and thereby opens up a whole new market for the company's products.

  * By placing a review of a new book into the knowledge network, an accountant helps others identify a valuable resource or warns others against wasting their time and money purchasing the book.

  * By reviewing a course taken at a local college, or from a professional society, a secretary helps others plan their own learning activities.

Conclusion: Breaking Out of the Boundaries

The beauty of the knowledge network is that these types of connections occur even when the person making the entry in the network doesn't know who else could benefit from the information or idea. The true value of the information surpasses the conventional boundaries that often restrict employees' thinking. The call center representative may not know anyone in the marketing department, but when she places the customer's idea into the marketing discussion forum someone from marketing is certain to see it. By placing a paper given by a competitor at a conference into the knowledge network, people in marketing or research or sales get ideas for new products or better ways to position products and services. The possibilities are endless. But they can come about only if (1) the information is placed into the network, (2) employees have the tools to easily find the information, and (3) employees use the network on a regular basis.

Notes

1. Thomas H. Davenport, "Teltech: The Business of Knowledge Management Case Study," Graduate School of Business, University of Texas at Austin, 1996.
2. Ibid.
3. Michael A. Verespej, "Skills on Call," *Industry Week*, CompuServe Online edition, June 3, 1996.
4. Ibid.
5. John Mariotti, "The Right Mix of Technology," *Industry Week*, CompuServe Online edition, December 16, 1996.
6. George Taninecz, "What Went Wrong?" *Industry Week*, CompuServe Online edition, December 16, 1996.
7. John Teresko, "Connecting R&D to the Market," *Industry Week*, CompuServe Online edition, December 16, 1996.
8. "Jack Welch's Encore," *Business Week*, October 28, 1996, p. 155.
9. Management Forum for Excellence in Software Development, "Information Package."

Afterword: The Knowledge-Enabled Organization and the Future

> A unique characteristic of knowledge is that it is one of the few assets that grows most—usually exponentially—when shared.
>
> James Brian Quinn, *Intelligent Enterprise,*
> The Free Press

Creating a knowledge-enabled organization is a prerequisite for any company's future success. There is no function, no job within any company today, regardless of industry or location, that is not knowledge-based. At the same time, the amount of knowledge that employees at all levels need to do their jobs is expanding exponentially; in the future no employee will be able to master all of the knowledge needed to do a job. The best that we can do for our employees is to build a positive learning environment where they are engaged in continuous learning and can use knowledge networks to gather and share the knowledge they need to succeed individually and collectively.

Just as scientists say that human beings use only a small fraction of the potential of their brains, so companies today use only a small fraction of the knowledge and skills resources contained within their own boundaries. The company must be seen as a living organism, one that manages its own well-being and responds to its external environments (customers, suppliers, competitors, and markets). Valery Kanevsky of Hewlett-Packard and University of Southern California Professor Tom Housel believe that companies must learn from each and every market transaction: "When a customer purchases our product, she changes the market forever. Corporate success largely rests on the ability to translate learning from these changes into knowledge that will result in new or modified products."[1]

This conviction follows the learning model presented in Chapter 2: The information from the market is transformed into knowledge only when it is applied to the work of the company (in the instance above, to make changes in products and marketing strategies). Kanevsky and Housel go further to state that the market "organism" is similar to other living creatures, responding to stimulation and activity by learning and adapting. Furthermore, it must also take an organic approach, adapting to changing markets: "Learning is a critical element in ensuring that our corporation makes the necessary adjustments to the new market environment by continuing to produce valuable products."[2]

No single approach to becoming a knowledge-enabled organization works for all companies. This book purposefully presents various approaches, tried by companies that differ in size, industry, markets, and locations, in the hope that you will find some ideas of value to your situation. Consider this view from Tom Davenport, a business professor and pioneer in knowledge management:

> But now the new frontier is in our minds. As free natural resources and cheap labor are exhausted, the last untapped source of commercial advantage is the knowledge of people in organizations. It is very early days for knowledge management. . . . The good news is that almost anything that a firm does in managing knowledge will be a step forward.[3]

In today's dynamic global business environment, learning isn't an option. Companies that learn to harness the knowledge and skills of their employees, build a positive learning environment, and become a knowledge-enabled organization can build a prosperous future, for the future itself is little more than a learning process. As British futurist Graham May sees it:

> Regarding the future as dynamic and uncertain can be threatening, but it can also be exciting and liberating. There is always something new to be created or discovered. Learning is less a matter of acquiring a fixed body of knowledge and more a search for the new; it is the development of capabilities to create our future, rather than foresee what is predetermined.[4]

The journey to becoming a knowledge-enabled organization seems chaotic at times, but it is always exciting. The benefits to your company can be great. For your employees, being a part of a knowledge-enabled organization makes each new day a challenge, one they continually seek because they sense their own growth within a dynamic and prosperous organization. This excitement about the future is plainly evident at those companies that have begun the journey. Your company can discover that excitement, too.

Notes

1. Valery Kanevsky and Tom Housel, "The Learning-Knowledge-Value Cycle: Tracking the Velocity of Change in Knowledge to Value," undated conference paper.
2. Ibid.
3. Thomas H. Davenport, "Some Principles of Knowledge Management," working paper, University of Texas at Austin, 1996.
4. Graham H. May, "The Future as a Learning Process." Originally appeared in the July-August 1996 issue of THE FUTURIST, p. 60. Used with permission from the World Future Society, 7910 Woodmont Avenue, Suite 450, Bethesda, Maryland 20814. (301) 656-8274; fax (301) 951-0394.

Index of Companies

Index